A NEW WAY TO KNOW

Using Artificial Intelligence to Augment
Learning in Students with Cognitive Disabilities

AL JONES, JR., ED.D.

leverage in **learning**

A New Way to Know: Using Artificial Intelligence to Augment Learning in Students with Cognitive Disabilities

Published by Leverage in Learning
www.leverageinlearning.com
Contact: info@leverageinlearning.com

Printed in the United States of America

For permissions, bulk orders, or bookings, please address correspondence to: info@leverageinlearning.com

ISBN: 978-1-7354534-0-8 (print)

DEDICATION

This book is dedicated to

D. D. L. for engaging in endless conversations and providing unwavering support in the writing of this book

and

to my wonderful and loving parents,

Rev. Dr. A. C. Jones, Sr. & Dorothy Wood Jones.

ABBREVIATIONS

AI   Artificial intelligence

CD   Cognitive disability

CSR   Corporate social responsibility

ESSA   Every Student Succeeds Act

IDEA   Individuals with Disabilities Education Act

IEP   Individualized Education Plan

IQ   Intelligence quotient

SES   Socioeconomic status

TABLE OF CONTENTS

INTRODUCTION

No heat, lights turned off and no hot water occurred occasionally at home during my childhood. Looking back during that time, I would say my family was working-class poor. Early on in my childhood, my father lost his job. He highlighted during an interview for a promotion that he was the president of a local NAACP chapter and he was not able to find another job after that incident. However, rather than let that stop him, he started his own business as a contractor. To this day, I am amazed that he never let that whole situation make him a bitter man. He found a way to move forward despite what life threw at him and always treated everyone with love and respect. Over time, my family fluctuated from working-class poor to lower-middle class. Through everything, I never once thought of myself as poor; we just did not have money. My family was rich with all the things we needed: a close, loving family, a safe home, kindness, laughter and love. Reflections on my childhood are filled with countless fond memories. I grew up with my mother, father, and two younger sisters in Richmond, Virginia. I was blessed to have a mother who was there to see me off to school and greet me when I came home every day, as my mother was a stay-at-home mom until I entered high school. My father was a Baptist minister in the Charlottesville, Virginia area. Because we lived in Richmond, every weekend we would put on our Sunday best, load ourselves into the station wagon, and make the one-hour drive to and from Charlottesville for church. Eventually, the church at which my father served as the pastor rented a house, which was a beautiful rancher that was beside the church. After that point, we would spend the entire weekend in Charlottesville, come back Sunday night, and get ready for school on Monday. Because of that, I always thought of the weekends as a middle-class get-away filled with love and family.

To say that my parents were big on education would be the understatement of the century. They were *extremely* big on education, constantly extoling its importance and how it was the key to a successful life. One of the core values of our home was that all the children were expected to study and work hard in school, and this was a value that had been deeply ingrained in us from as early as we could remember.

One of the primary reasons that my mother and my father had decided when my siblings and I were born that my mother would be a stay-at-home mom is so that she could keep us keenly focused on education. Thus, every day when we came home from school, after a warm greeting, a hug, a snack, and changing out of our school clothes, my mother would sit down with us at the dining room table and go over our homework with us every single day. Participation in this daily homework huddle was a residential requirement of every child in our household. There were no options and rarely any exceptions. For instance, I remember one winter when the furnace was out because the gas was cut off, and our house was *cold*. Absolutely frigid! Although I didn't enjoy the cutting chill of the house, in my mind, there was a silver lining: *At least there's no way we're going to have to do any homework or studying today. It's too cold!* Boy, was I wrong! We still had to do homework, because in our house, education came first, no matter what. No excuses. I also recall that soon after that, my father put in a wood stove to take care of heating the house so we wouldn't run into anymore furnace issues interrupting our study time. My parents might not have had all of the money or material goods that they would have liked to have given us, but they always ensured that my siblings and I had all that we needed for school, no matter what.

My parents' heavy emphasis on education and its virtues was effectively transferred down to us kids. We understood their message clearly: education is *everything*. Thus, doing well in school was a no-brainer in our household. There was no "You do well in school, or else!" There was simply, "You do well in school. Period!" As I fondly reflect on those days sitting around the dining room table with textbooks, homework handouts, and writing tablets spread out before us while we diligently studied our lessons, I recall that my sisters were always better students than me. However, I worked hard and held my own as a solid "B" student.

There was never a moment in my life in which I thought my education would not include college. In our household, and in my own mind, college was a part of the natural progression of getting an education. After elementary school, middle school was not an option. After middle school, high school was not an option. After high school, college was not an option. There were no "Ifs" about college; it was only a matter of "Where" and "How" I was going to go to college.

Individuals are made up of different defining moments in their lives that shape who they are. One of the most significant moments of this sort for me was the day that my family dropped me off at Howard University to begin my freshman year. "What's so 'defining' about this moment that millions of other freshmen also experience each year?" you might ask. The reason it was defining for me was that only hours before we reached the Howard University campus in Washington, D.C., I was sitting at home in Richmond, Virginia, thinking that I wasn't going to be able to go to college.

Here's what I knew as a solid fact: college required money. Here's another thing that I knew: my family didn't have any money. I had done my part as a student: I had applied to the university and gotten accepted. However, in order to enroll for the fall semester, I had to register for my classes and pay the tuition, or at least a part of it. Guess what. We didn't have *any* of it! Two weeks before classes were scheduled to begin, out of nowhere, my father walked into my bedroom and told me to pack my things because he was about to take me to college. I looked at him quizzically with wonder and bewilderment. *What is this man thinking? Did he forget that you have to pay to enroll for classes?* I thought. However, I did as I was told (because this is how I was raised) and hurriedly packed my things into two classic foot locker trunks that had been sitting in my room for a year. Looking back now, I think my folks had planned for me to use the trunks for college all along.

As my father and I went back and forth from the house to the car loading my things, I couldn't help but ask him the questions that were weighing on my mind, questions that I thought to be very relevant considering the circumstances. First and foremost, I asked, "But Dad, how are we going to pay for college?" No answer. Then, I began trying to negotiate with my father in order to introduce some reason and rationality into what seemed to me like an irrational and haphazard attempt to finagle me into Howard University's freshman class. "Dad, it's no problem. I can just go to school later!" I pleaded. Still, no answer. My father just kept packing my things, squeezing them into wherever they would fit in the car and leaving just enough room for my mother, sisters and me. The only thing my father said was, "Let's go now. I insist. We're going." I can't even begin to tell you how anxious and uneasy that two-hour car ride was. Every part of me expected to be taking the same route in reverse hours later, disappointed that the university wouldn't allow me to enroll based on a promise to pay some time in the future and a prayer.

When we pulled up to the beautiful historic Howard University campus, my heart leaped! My father went directly to the registrar's office, and I waited, taking in the sights of a campus that was abuzz with smiling students. I watched as young co-eds bumped into each other after the summer off and cheerfully greeted each other with warm hugs. I watched as parents unloaded their kids' luggage, bedding, laundry baskets, and foot lockers and then entered the dorms to help them set up their rooms. All the while, I wished it was happening to me.

After about an hour, my father emerged from the building that housed the registrar's office. "Okay. You're enrolled," he said. He said it so casually and with an air of nonchalance that I had him repeat it. "What?" I asked. "You're enrolled!" he said. "Now let's go get your things and get you moved in." I was shocked and speechless! As we walked back to the car, my mind continued trying to put two and two together, but nothing was adding up. I knew that we didn't have the money, but I was enrolled. How could this be? I couldn't figure out what my father could have possibly told them for them to agree to enroll me, but they did! My family and I went back to the car, drove around to Drew Hall (the freshman male dorm), and unloaded my things. During the whole time we were in Washington, D.C., the car had to be left running parked on the street on Georgia Avenue. If it was turned off, it wouldn't start again, and it would have to be jumped or even possibly towed. Thus, there was no time for long goodbyes with my family. As soon as the last of my items touched the floor in my room, they made an immediate departure. It was just as well; I needed some time alone to process the whirlwind of events that had just happened to me. Only hours before, I was sitting in my bedroom at home in Richmond, and now, here I was, a 17-year-old kid enrolled in college. I sat on my bed, looked around my room, and shook my head in disbelief as I thought about how much life is filled with unexpected – yet very welcome – twists and turns!

Once I overcame the shock and incredulity that I was now living the dream as an officially-enrolled freshman at Howard University, something else set in: an overwhelming sense of determination. I came to the stark realization that this was my chance – my only chance – and that if I didn't seize it, I would never get this chance again. I knew that this would be a journey filled with various unknown obstacles, but at that moment, I determined that whatever was thrown at me, I would overcome, no matter what. I was determined to work hard, do well in my classes, and help relieve some of the financial burden on my family along the way. They had sacrificed so much for me all my life, and I wanted to do what I could to take some of the pressure of paying for college off of them.

I recall the summer following my freshman year at Howard, I went back home to Richmond. My father asked me what I was planning to do for the summer, and I told him I was going to get a job to make some money. On the weekends, when my father was not ministering to his congregation in Charlottesville, his regular nine-to-five job was his business as a general contractor. He thought that instead of going out to find another job, I should work with him doing general contract work. I accepted the invitation. That summer was absolutely horrible. My father worked me like a *slave*! The summer heat, plus working outdoors, plus the hard physical labor was more than I'd bargained for when I'd accepted his job offer. In fact, my father worked me so hard that I resolved that I would never go back home for summer break ever again! I kind of think that he did this deliberately, almost as an effort to haze me and teach me a lesson about finishing my education so I wouldn't have to do this kind of work for a living in the future. I had already resolved to do whatever it took to finish my degree, but this summer, working outdoors with my father under the intense July heat had sealed the deal. I knew that I only had one chance to make college work. I had to make the most of my situation at Howard and not blow the opportunity to get a degree, because this would be the pathway toward a better life. Going back home empty-handed wasn't an option.

Almost immediately after enrolling at Howard University, I registered for the work study program, and I worked there from my first year all the way through to graduation. As I watched my friends come in, go out, and enjoy their work-free lives, I would think, *Man... they look like they're having so much fun.* Nevertheless, I stuck to the plan and did what I had to do, working hard to juggle academics and my work study assignments. Fun was one thing, but I wasn't going to quit working and not get done what needed to be done. That's not to say that I didn't enjoy my campus experience. Quite the opposite is true; I thoroughly enjoyed my friends and social life in college and had a lot of fun. I just didn't have as much free time as my counterparts who didn't have to work to make ends meet.

I forged ahead, and five years later, in 1993, my hard work and strong resolve paid off: I graduated with a Bachelor of Arts in Telecommunications Management. I had chosen Telecommunications Management when I'd originally applied to Howard, but unlike many other students, I'd stuck to the same major all the way through school. I knew I was skilled in working with people, in writing, and in communicating, and I thought that this particular major was the best way to harness all of my skills and talents. Ultimately, my plan was to work in television, possibly getting a job working for the TV networks or in some position related to broadcasting. After completing my bachelor's degree at Howard, the very first job I took was in broadcasting as an intern at NBC. There, I did general intern work like writing community interest stories, doing research for various stories, etc. The schedule wasn't the best; there were lots of rotating shifts and inconsistent hours. Before I'd graduated from Howard, I already knew that I was going to go to graduate school. Once I started the intern job with the crazy hours, I realized that a work schedule that didn't allow for set workdays and hours wouldn't fit with me being able to take graduate classes. Besides that, I discovered that the person who had been working in the same job role before I came along only lasted a couple of months. Learning this sent up a whole new set of red flags. I knew that as much as media interested me, I needed to find another job to support myself. Little did I know, all these things were working together to point me towards a different course that I had never considered before. A new career loomed on the horizon!

I accepted a job substitute teaching, a move that would change my entire career focus and trajectory forever. While substitute teaching in Prince George's County, Maryland, I fell in love with education... but it was more than that. I was working with special education students in the classroom, and I fell in love with them as individuals – a group of people who actually needed assistance and that allowed me to see the direct benefits of my instruction on their lives. I was hooked! I decided to pursue a Master of Arts in Special Education at Bowie State University (about an hour northeast of D.C.), a degree which focused on the transition of individuals with disabilities from educational settings into the workplace. After this, in 2003, I completed an Ed.D. in Education from The George Washington University in Washington, D.C. with a focus on special education.

In between my master's and my doctorate, I completed my Ed.S. degree, which included interning at The National Association of

State Directors of Special Education as a part of the program. It was working there that I fell in love with policy administration. I found that when you work in policy, you can change the course of how education is delivered and shape the ways in which it affects millions of students. Being able to affect change in the lives of individuals one-on-one on the classroom level was stimulating, but being able to shape the educational system on a state level was downright *electrifying*! I became captivated with the challenge of working through policy issues and coming up with solutions that would best meet the needs of the students we served.

From there, my new passion was clear, and my career course was set. I knew that I would dedicate my life and career to working in special education, helping to make a positive impact on the lives of those who are a part of this special community. People ask me how I could go from telecommunications management and end up working with special education. That's easy: I went where I had the most passion and skill in order to be able to make the most impact. At the intersection of these components lay a highly-rewarding and profoundly-satisfying career that I have enjoyed for the past 27 years, and I am deeply grateful.

I can truly say that at every step of my career in special education, I learned and experienced things that contributed to me becoming more and more deeply vested in serving children with cognitive disabilities. For example, after substitute teaching in a high school in Prince George's County, MD, I worked in a middle school setting as an intervention specialist on a special education wing for kids who had emotional disturbances. Back then, special education was not as integrated or mainstreamed as it is today, so rather than work with the kids in the classroom, my job was to pull them out of their special education class to address their needs. Most of the time, they had difficulty controlling and managing their emotions, and this impacted their learning. After removing them from the classroom, my objective was to identify what triggered their sad or angry emotional outburst, teach them how to identify these triggers so they could avoid them in the future, get them back into an emotional state in which they could continue learning, and take them back to the classroom.

I have been a staunch supporter and advocate for the CD community for decades. Not only do I have a M.A. in Special Education and an Ed.D. in Education, but I have worked in the field for more than 25 years. My educational career journey has taken me from working in the classroom, to working in the National Association of State Directors of Special Education, to working in the U.S. Department of Education, where I am tasked with ensuring that states comply with federal laws surrounding education.

In every phase of my educational career, I have been passionately driven by the goal of improving the educational and post-educational outcomes of students with CD. I have witnessed the lackluster instructional practices and the poor learning outcomes they have produced. I have heard the stories that desperate parents have pleaded with me to listen to about how much more their cognitively-disabled children could accomplish in the classroom if the teacher were to step out of the box and simply do whatever it takes to get their children to learn. I have reviewed the research, read the reports, seen the statistics and shaken my head at how poorly we fare in providing the best education possible to students with CD. At some point, I decided that I could either sit by and wait for someone else to initiate the conversation about how to innovate the instruction we offer to students with CD, or I could broach such discussions myself. I chose the latter. Thus, this book was born.

My Purpose and Vision for This Book

In my research and experience, I have found artificial intelligence to be one of the most critical factors in increasing learning outcomes for students with CD. Although there is still a lack of consensus among those in the field about how to define artificial intelligence, one of the most well-respected technical descriptions and definitions of artificial intelligence is published in the Journal of Artificial Intelligence:[1]

> The essence of intelligence is the principle of adapting to the environment while working with insufficient knowledge and resources. Accordingly, an intelligent system should rely on finite processing capacity, work in real time, open to unexpected tasks, and learn from experience. This working definition interprets "intelligence" as a form of "relative rationality."[2]

If that definition seems a bit complex, the following is a more layman's definition:[3]

> Artificial intelligence (AI), also known as machine intelligence, is a branch of computer science that aims to imbue software with the ability to analyze its environment using either predetermined rules and search algorithms, or pattern recognizing machine learning models, and then make decisions based on those analyses.

If I were to break it down even further for a friend unfamiliar with the concept, I would simply describe artificial intelligence as: technology that is developed to mimic the thinking and reasoning processes of the human brain.

Regardless of which definition you prefer, you should know that AI is not a dream far off in the future; it is currently being engaged in the here and now. AI is being used in some amazing, innovative ways to help humans accomplish the most complex tasks and achieve objectives at a fraction of the time and with exponentially-greater levels of accuracy than we ever imagined. The good news is, just when our minds are blown by the new latest and greatest thing AI can do to benefit our lives, another development is revealed that leaves us speechless in wonder. The field of AI is vast. The more we learn about it, the more we recognized that the potential for AI development exceeds the limits of what the human mind can imagine.

I wrote this book for the purpose of introducing conversations about AI being integrated into the instructional cycle and to spark immediate action among parents, educators and policymakers. As you read through the pages, you will see that I will present a lot of questions that are meant to spark critical conversations. However, even though I raise a lot of questions, let me tell you now that I do not have all of the answers. There's a lot of fleshing out of details that will need to occur before we can fully implement the shift towards the use of AI-augmented learning in educating students with CD that I am proposing. However, in the meantime, while these conversations are being held, decisions are being made, and policies are being fleshed out, I will show you how we can start where we are. The amazing, never-before-seen ways in which artificial intelligence can benefit the educational outcomes of students with disabilities is not something that can wait! Thus, I also propose some actional steps that readers can take to begin the process of implementing the shift.

My vision for this book is to change the minds of readers about the need to make a shift in how we educate students with CD so that they can achieve better educational and post-educational outcomes and to leave readers convinced that AI-augmented learning is the way to do it. The fulfillment of this vision will look like people reading all the way through the book, and at the end, closing the book with their minds spinning about what they will do to tell everyone in their sphere of influence about how AI-augmented learning is something we must adopt. I envision turning every reader into an advocate for AI technology in education, so if it seems like I'm trying to sway you over to seeing things my way as I write, I am! I need people like you to stand with me as advocates for making a shift towards AI-augmented learning, positioning education at the leading edge of AI innovation. If we work together, we can help to improve the educational and post-educational success of these students, and in the process, benefit us as a society.

This book is written for parents and educators of children with cognitive disabilities. Perhaps you are a parent who just found out that your child has a cognitive disability and you are concerned about whether there is hope for your child to perform at or above the level of his or her peers. Maybe you're a parent who has known for years that your child has a cognitive disability, and you have had to stand by and witness the constant challenges that your child has had to face in the classroom. You've had to wipe the tears, speak soothing words to calm the frustration, give the encouraging pep talks, and keep your child motivated to keep going, even when the last thing they wanted was to walk back into that school.

If you're like most parents who have dealt with having a student with CD long-term, your greatest concern is not for today but for tomorrow: will your child be able to take care of him or herself when they finish school? Will they be able to live as a functional adult on their own? And then, there's the biggest looming question of them all: if anything happens to you or your spouse and there's no one to care for your child, will your child be sufficiently prepared to care for him or herself? These are the questions that keep you up at night. These are the very questions – the ones about the potentials for tomorrow – that drive you to advocate for better educational practices in the classroom to-day. For you, making a difference and improving the education-al and post-educational outcomes of your child is about life or death. Thus, you didn't just pick up this book for a good read. It's personal for you.

It is also written with technology companies in mind, particu-larly those that are racing forward to make innovations in the artificial intelligence space.

My Hopes for You as a Reader of This Book

I penned this book with some very specific hopes in mind, all centered on improving the lives of those who occupy a unique, undervalued and often misunderstood space in our society – the special education community. Until now, individuals with CD might have represented a population that has not registered on your radar as important. You might even consider them irrel-evant. However, I aim to change your perception of this special community, because whether you realize it or not, you occupy different spaces within the same society, so your life is inex-tricably intertwined with theirs. Thus, it is important that you view them in the right light. This fundamental hope underlies each of the following specific hopes I have for you as a reader of this book.

First, my hope for you as a reader of this book is for you to first understand that the educational and post-educational outcomes of students with CD affect all of us. It's not an issue that is simply relegated to the parents, families and teachers of students with CD. These individuals' preparation for life after school – or lack thereof – has a direct social and economic impact on our com-munities. Thus, innovating CD education is something in which each and every one of us should take an immediate interest.

Second, my hope is that every reader of this book will realize that the success of students with CD is our community's success. Communities are not made up of individuals or pockets of people who exist in isolation from the rest of the group. We're all in the same community together, interconnected. Each individual and subgroup of the community acts upon and influences the rest of the community, and vice versa. Thus, none of us can afford to turn a blind eye to inequities affecting any other group of the community, because ultimately, their outcomes will have an impact on us in some way and at some time.

Next, it is my hope that after you finish reading this book, you will not simply lay it aside and say, "Hmmm... that was an interesting book!" If that's all that happens, I have failed in my mission. This book is designed to spur you to action, for you to add your voice to the collective expression of discontent about how students with CD are educated in our school systems today.

Finally, it is my hope to move you, as a reader of this book, from a position of silent observer to one of outspoken advocate. It is my aim to transform you into a supporter of school systems doing whatever it takes to increase educational and post-educational outcomes for students with CD. If you are a parent, this looks like recognizing that there is an opportunity for change and adding your signature, voice, and presence to any efforts undertaken to advance this mission. If you are an administrator, this looks like carefully considering the possibilities of implementing the ideas in this book in the learning environments that you manage and oversee. If you are a teacher, this looks like thinking about what needs to be adjusted and making the use of the ideas presented in this book as beneficial as possible to the students in CD classrooms. Finally, if you are a policymaker, this looks like recognizing that this conversation has policy implications as much as it has individual implications for students and introducing new policy mandates aimed towards innovating the ways in which we instruct and assess students with CD in the classroom.

It is an unfortunate reality that the amazing members of the CD community exist in a world where inequality tends to be the norm and equity usually comes with a steep price tag that few individuals can pay. I wield the strength of my ideas with the hope that they will spark you and others to consider new ways of looking at how we can effectively serve this community, engaging you in a collective effort that will ultimately affect real, lasting change in their lives. If I can, through the pages of this book, initiate ideas that grow into initiatives that meet and exceed the needs of one of the most underrated and undervalued populations in America, all of the investments that I have made into this project will be worthwhile.

CARLOS'S STORY

Carlos is in elementary school, and he has a moderate cognitive disability. Mr. Thomas, Carlos's teacher, and Mrs. Jackson, the special education teacher, have worked with Carlos to learn numbers and count to 100. Carlos's next big challenge is to learn addition, subtraction, multiplication, and division. Carlos is in class with his classmates who do not have disabilities and gets the same math lessons that they do. But, in addition to those lessons, Carlos is systematically taught how to perform math calculations on a calculator. Mr. Thomas and Mrs. Jackson are delighted to find that Carlos, with the aid of the calculator, can complete the same math problems his non-disabled peers complete. While not an easy task, Carlos has learned to recognize which type of math problem requires which type of calculator function. The early success of Carlos has given him the desire to engage in more math problems. Working more math problems creates a cycle of increased practice and success, which has helped Carlos progress with his peers.

This is the power of AI in education.

WHAT'S SO FUNNY?
Cognitive Disability

The fact that you're reading this book is an indication of the strong likelihood that you went to elementary, middle and high school. Over all of those years walking through the hallways of your schools, you've probably seen a special education classroom or two, and you've seen the unique types of students that tend to fill these classrooms. Thus, you probably already have a clear mental image of what students with cognitive disabilities tend to look like and how they tend to function. You and your friends probably referred to them as the "special needs" kids. However, what does it mean for a student to be special in this way, or to have a cognitive disability? This is the first among many questions that we must answer before moving ahead.

First, you should understand that cognitive disability and intellectual disability, although closely related, are not the same. The concepts can be defined in the following ways:

Cognitive Disability

Cognition refers to one's general awareness and points specifically to his/her basic ability to learn. Thus, cognitive disabilities are obstacles that individuals have in learning. Their challenges might include one or a number of difficulties like understanding, processing, recognizing, perceiving, remembering, and choosing content or information, but they can also include the lack of ability to focus for an extended amount of time or to retain what they are taught in their short-term memory. Any time a student has something blocking his/her learning progress or thought process, the student is considered to have a cognitive disability.[4] Cognitive disabilities appear before 22 years old and will more than likely challenge the individual for the rest of his/her life.[5]

Intellectual Disability

Intelligence refers to one's fundamental ability to acquire and utilize knowledge, leveraging it in a manner suitable for the situation. Thus, intellectual disabilities are a specific category of challenges to general cognitive functioning that result in a lower intelligence quotient (IQ) and introduce substantial challenges in students' social skills and how they adapt to new contexts or situations.[6] Such challenges can include classroom difficulties like impeding their ability to take an exam, and general adaptive abilities like being able to socialize with others, handle concepts like money and time, engage in social problem solving, follow rules and laws, adhere to schedules and routines, and manage their own personal care.[7] These chronic and often severe limitations in intellectual functioning, and in adaptive behavior originate before an individual is 18 years old and usually require them to receive intensive support over a lifetime. Formerly, the term "mental retardation" was used to refer to this population.

However, advocates promote the use of "intellectual disability" as the preferred term to refer to these individuals.[8]

Second, it's not enough to understand each of the individual constructs; we must understand their connection. Here's the relationship between cognitive and intellectual disability: intellectual disability is a condition that is clinically diagnosed based on deficits in cognitive and adaptive functioning during childhood and adolescent years.[9] The defining characteristics of intellectual disability are cognitive and adaptive functioning deficits. In light of our understanding of the differences between the two concepts, it is possible for a student who has an exceptionally high IQ to have extreme cognitive disabilities. For example, in the case of a child simultaneously having high intelligence and cognitive disabilities:

> This child may be amazing at counting objects or doing advanced math, such as can occur in some forms of autism or attention deficit disorder. Yet, he or she can be painfully disabled in his or her ability to function in a traditional learning environment due to a constant reversing of letters, inability to process written language, or concentrate for more than a moment on a task.[10]

Understanding this should help to dispel one of the biggest myths and remove one of the strongest biases that you and others might have about students in special education classes: they can be *extremely* intelligent. Many of them can have a higher IQ than their non-special education peers. What has landed them in a special education class is not their lack of intelligence but obstacles that hinder their ability to learn.

Cognitive disabilities are not monolithic; they cover the range of a spectrum that begins with "mild" and ends with "severe."

- **Mild cognitive disability** – Accounts for around 85% of all cognitive disabilities. Children in this category have IQ scores between 55 and 70 and are usually included in the mainstream classroom.

- **Moderate cognitive disability** – Accounts for 10% of all cognitive disabilities. Children in this category have IQ scores between 30 and 55.

- **Severe cognitive disability** – Accounts for 3-4% of all cognitive disabilities. Children in this category have IQ scores that fall under 30 and will have few communication skills. Because of their diminished capacity to function independently, they will need direct supervision.

Cognitive disabilities can manifest in many forms. Several of the most common types of cognitive disabilities include the following severe and less severe cognitive conditions.

More severe cognitive conditions:

- Down syndrome
- Traumatic brain injury
- Autism
- Dementia

Less severe cognitive conditions:

- Dyslexia
- Attention Deficit Disorder
- Dyscalculia
- Other learning disabilities

Cognitive disabilities affect every part of what an individual needs to be able to function independently in any stage of life. The deficiencies in their mental functioning hinders their judgment, memory, perception, planning, speech, social skills, and their ability to engage in sound decision making and problem solving.[11] As a result, individuals with CD live under a stigma that results in a life marked by marginalization, discrimination, social exclusion, and in the worst cases, abuse. There is no part of these individuals' lives that goes unimpacted by the stigma that accompanies having a cognitive disability. Every domain of their existence, ranging from education to community integration, from health, hygiene and reproductive rights to finances, and from intimate relationships to personal safety is adversely affected by their condition.[12]

The Most Difficult Diagnosis:
Learning Your Child Has a Cognitive Disability

Embracing a diagnosis that your child has a cognitive disability is one of the most difficult realities that any parent can face. The moment that they receive such news, a complex journey towards acceptance begins. The first step on the journey: mourning. During the mourning process, parents must adjust to the idea that they have a child with disabilities and adjust all of the hopes, dreams and expectations they once had of their child to that of a new norm. Then, over time, they gradually begin to accept that this is real and it's not going away. You know that they've truly embraced the reality of their child's cognitive disability when they begin to proactively advocate for what is best for the child in skills development and learning.

Parents who have reached acceptance rely on the educational process to meet their child's need and set their expectations for milestone completion based on norms commensurate with the progress of a special needs child rather than on norms for a child without special needs. They recognize that their child will learn, but because the basis of learning is cognition and their child is at a cognitive disadvantage, their child's learning outcomes may not meet or exceed the outcomes of children without a cognitive disability. Of course, there are parents who never adjust their expectations based upon their child's disability. These are the ones that I talk to the most, the ones that tend to make the most noise in the school system.

If you ask parents about what life is like having a child with CD, they will tell you that they love their children more than anything in the world, but having a child with CD is definitely a struggle. For every significant milestone reached, there seems to be a setback that causes them great concern. For every new skill mastered, there seems to be a whole new set of supplemental micro-skills to master in order to sustain the big new skill. For every two steps taken forward, there seems to be one step taken backward. Having a child with CD is amazing and rewarding, but it's also hard. Parents want you to know that.

Everyone's Favorite Punchline: The Social Stigma and Low Social Regard for Individuals with Cognitive Disabilities

The current social view of individuals with cognitive disabilities is not a positive one. Despite the many advancements made among this population, those who fall into it are still highly stigmatized. Individuals with cognitive disabilities, are the most undervalued population in our society. As a result, society has grown accustomed to making fun of individuals with cognitive disabilities. In fact, mocking and ridiculing individuals with cognitive disabilities has become so normalized and commonplace that when jokes are made about them, we chuckle rather than gasp in shame or horror about their inappropriateness. Jokes about special education students and people with lower cognitive functioning prevail throughout television and social media, and very rarely will anyone step up to rebuke these jokesters or express disdain at the cheap shots and uncreative jabs that target these individuals as their victims. I can't emphasize enough the mental narrowness, the inhumanity, and the lack of basic empathy that this demonstrates about those who seek to bring shame and ridicule to people in the cognitive disability community. It's just plain cruel. They hear the jokes that comedians tell from national platforms, see others laughing, and understand that they are punchlines. It doesn't feel good to them.

One of the things that bothers me most is that we treat the disabled population this way with our kids watching. They pick up on every negative view that adults have about their peers with cognitive disabilities, and because of this, they feel comfortable ridiculing their CD peers themselves. After all, why would they think they would get in trouble for doing the same thing they see their parents and other influential adults doing? It is true that children are going to be children; they will always find some reason to tease their classmates, even those without CD. However, we cannot expect our children to do better towards this population if we, the adults, don't do better. We've got to set a better example for them that makes them think twice about mercilessly ridiculing students with CD, teaching them empathy instead.

When you look at a person with a cognitive disability, remember that there's still a human being in there. They are real people who think, process, love, have hopes, dreams and aspirations just like everyone else. They have hearts and they have feelings. They experience hurt, pain, fear and shame just like you and I do. They find things funny and tell jokes. They have personalities. The only difference between CD and non-CD people is that individuals with CD may need additional help to function. Trust me, if people with CD could be self-sufficient and do things on their own, they would do so, and gladly. They would love to do all of the things we who do not have CD do and take for granted. Whether those with CD have profound disabilities (because there is a CD spectrum) and need a lot of extra help to function or they are at the lighter end of the spectrum, given the right amount of assistance, they all can thrive.

As a society, I think we can do so much better in our regard and treatment of those with CD. In fact, I know we can. Part of my advocacy for this community is helping people to look at someone with CD and see a boy, girl, man, or woman who is, first and foremost, a human being just like them. Don't see the disability first. See the person first, not the disability. Treat them like a human being worthy of compassion and respect. Even if we just start with this, we'll be doing better towards people in the CD community.

"I Know My Child Can Do More!": Parents' Concerns About the Education of Their Children with Cognitive Disabilities

As an education program specialist, I talked directly to a lot of parents. I recall one mother, in particular, whose son was in the 9th grade. She called my office and wanted to talk because she didn't agree with his Individualized Education Plan (IEP), which is a plan that outlines the school's goals for providing specialized instruction and support for students with CD. She had reviewed the IEP that the school had recently sent home for her son, and she was upset because she said that his goals in high school were the same ones that he'd had on his IEP in elementary school. Besides this, she didn't see how the goals on his IEP would help him in life. She felt that his school wasn't truly interested in educating her son. In fact, she said that our special education was simply "glorified babysitting." She had already taken her concerns to the school administration, and the officials said that she was being unrealistic about her son's educational progress and potential. To add insult to injury, they also labeled her as an angry parent, absolving themselves of the urgency to address her concerns. Despite her protests, they never changed her son's IEP. I remember her asking me, "How am I supposed to look out for my son if I can't get the school to do anything for him?" It was a very valid question, and it left me feeling trapped between a rock and a hard place. Ultimately, all I could do was tell her what the law said and advise her that she could request mediation, file a complaint, or pursue legal action to have her concerns addressed, but I don't think it actually fixed the problem. Her desperate appeal of "Please! Can you help me?" resonated in my ears and lay embedded in my conscience for years afterwards. It also identified a gap in the special education system and showed me that something needed to be done.

Over the years, I've talked to many parents who have used all of their economic resources to take the school system to court over such matters – and they've lost. Whether you realize it or not, if you have a complaint about the quality of education your child is receiving in a school's special education program and you want to sue them to see that changes are made, you're looking at spending anywhere from $50,000 to $100,000 in legal fees. Maybe more. There are advocates who will represent you for free in court, but there aren't enough of them to serve the people who need them. I don't have to tell you that most parents don't have the resources to fight their school system in court. Then again, even if you do have the resources to battle the school system in court and you get a favorable verdict, it really doesn't affect lasting change in the classroom. So what do concerned parents do? They try to be the loud, squeaky wheel as often as possible in order to ensure that their child receives more attention and is challenged at a greater level in the classroom. However, there's no real guarantee that this will happen.

The brick wall that parents find themselves crashing into when they demand that special education programs increase the quality of learning their children receive is the schools' commitment to preserving the status quo. Schools genuinely feel that they are doing the most they can do. They believe that the parents who criticize them for the lack of progress their children make in the classroom has more to do with the child than with the quality of instruction they receive. As quiet as it's kept, the truth is that most schools claim they have high expectations for all students, but they do not achieve high learning and academic outcomes for children with CD. They see these kids' cognitive disabilities as a limitation that will significantly restrict their level of functioning for the rest of their lives. That by some cruel permission of fate that allowed them to be born this way, they are inevitably doomed to exist in such a state, no matter how much classroom education they receive. Consequently, schools perceive that their hands are tied in the matter. They think, *How can we educate a child when it's physically impossible for the child to learn to the same standards as a child without a disability? What are we supposed to do, work a miracle? Parents think their kids are little geniuses and want too much from us. We'll just educate them to the best of our ability and leave it at that.*

The problem with this thinking is that human beings operate based on their level of expectation. If you, as a teacher or administrator, don't believe that a student can achieve certain milestones equal to those of children without CD, you will neither expect nor challenge them to do so. As a result, the quality of instruction that is delivered in most classrooms that serve students with CD is scaled down based on this diminished level of expectation. Schools say that their special needs students are being educated "to the best of their ability" but use a very low bar to define "best of their ability." This is especially concerning to parents, because in their eyes, their special needs children have vast potential and are capable of doing so much more than educators believe. They want the bar for what their children are expected to accomplish to be raised so that educators are held to a higher level of responsibility to produce better outcomes.

"I'm Afraid of What the Future Holds": The Greatest Cause for Concern for Parents of Children with CD

When I used to work in the classroom with students with CD, time after time I would listen to parents tell me about the stark contrasts between how their children fared at school versus how they performed at home. When they heard from their children's teachers, the teachers would tell them about all of the challenges the student was having in the classroom. There were countless stories of how poorly the child was scoring on assessments, difficulties with keeping up with the lesson, challenges with performing simple tasks, and so on. The parents would be perplexed when hearing this, because at home, the same child would be flourishing! They had a hard time reconciling how their son or daughter could be doing so well at home but having such a hard time accomplishing the same level of tasks at school. It was a real head-scratcher, and they would often request a meeting to talk to administration about such matters.

While I was in the classroom, I would occasionally have to deal with matters like this directly. After I left the classroom and began working in administration, I started hearing stories like this from every level of the educational system, from parents, to administrators, to policymakers. They all sounded the same: "The parent says their child does great at home, so it's clear the student has the capacity to perform. They can't figure out why the student is assessed so poorly at school!" I never dismissed any of them; I took each story at face value and believed every parent's account. Why did the skillsets that students with CD mastered in interactions at home disappear in the classroom? I added each narrative to the cache of data running in the background of my mind that my brain was using to try to crack the code of how we could better empower these students, helping them to thrive at school as well as their parents said they thrived at home.

In the process of analyzing what I had seen, heard and experienced, I came to some critical realizations. First, I realized that with the right circumstances and given the right accommodations, students with CD could excel in learning. It's not that they weren't capable of learning and functioning independently; the fact that they were able to master these things effectively at home was evidence of this. Thus, the issue with them failing to excel in the classroom had more to do with what was happening in the classroom than it had to do with them lacking the capacity to learn. Another realization that I came to was that although instruction occurred in both the classroom and in the home, the way parents taught their child and the way that teachers taught the child had to differ. Something about the parent's style of instruction helped the child to excel in learning. The fact that the teacher was not able to help the child excel in learning in the classroom suggested that the teacher's style and parent's style of teaching differed in some way.

Finally, I came to the conclusion that the difference between the parent's effective approach to instruction in the home and the teacher's ineffective approach to instruction in the school boiled down to one primary attitude: the teachers tended to stick to rigid "these are the rules of instruction" parameters defined by traditional teaching practices, while parents took a "whatever it takes" attitude. Parents were driven to help their cognitively-disabled children learn what they needed to learn in order to function and survive, even if their approaches seemed too accommodating, too out-of-the-box or too mentally crippling. They didn't care what they had to do; their child was going to learn, because for them, it was a matter of failure or survival.

As I considered each of these realizations, I realized that there were some significant instructional gaps in special education that needed to be addressed. However, these were gaps that no one seemed to be interested in addressing or paying any real attention. I was baffled. I felt it was abysmal that after three decades of working with special education students, we still had challenges providing instruction for children with cognitive disabilities. I felt there had to be a better way to do things. I began thinking, *What would change look like? How could we make change happen?* I was driven to fill the gap.

66 ⸻⸻⸻⸻⸻⸻⸻⸻⸻⸻⸻⸻

...I began thinking,
What would change look like?
How could we make change happen?
I was driven to fill the gap.

⸻⸻⸻⸻⸻⸻⸻⸻⸻⸻⸻⸻ **99**

The conflict that exists between parents of children with cognitive disabilities and the schools that are responsible for educating these kids has been an ongoing one for decades. Parents believe that their children have high learning potential and have the capacity to learn significantly more in the classroom, if only their children's learning challenges are recognized and adequately addressed in the classroom. Schools believe that they are doing the best they can, educating students with CD to the peak of what their individual cognition will allow. In the end, it really doesn't matter who's right or not. What really matters is that when most students with CD graduate from high school, they are only reading on a 3rd or 4th grade level. This is not an adequate reading and comprehension level for them to be able to take care of themselves, and their insufficient preparation to do for themselves should matter to each of us.

According to the most recent research on preparing students with CD for life after school, while efforts are being made to ensure that these students are prepared, more needs to be done, because what's being done is not enough. According to a recent report on measures that states should consider to better support the college and career readiness for students with disabilities:

> Despite progress in improving [college and career readiness] for students with disabilities, more effort is needed to ensure a greater number of students complete high school, enter postsecondary education, earn a degree or certificate, and find employment that leads to independence, self-sufficiency, and a living wage career.[13]

Here's my position. Yes, I believe that students with CD can learn more than they are currently learning in the classroom. And yes, I also believe that schools are doing the best they can in providing the best quality of education they can provide to these students, considering the status quo of special education delivery. I believe that the answer lies somewhere between the two positions. First, rather than accepting the status quo, educators need to focus on how to raise the bar for what "best of their abilities" means for students with CD. The purpose of this book is to propose how this can be accomplished through the integration of technology into special education classrooms.

My premise for the proposal is based on the idea that everyone can excel and maximize their individual capacity if given the right opportunities. People with CD are no different. The problem is, they are not given the support and opportunities that they need in their special education classrooms in order to make such achievements possible. If we dare to see the value resident in the many unique individuals of this community and meet them where they are rather than automatically devaluing their potential because they are not like us, we can affect some real change. We can push past the stigma and low expectations and provide them with what they need to excel in the classroom and in life.

Why We All Should Care About the Success of Cognitively-disabled Students

If you're not a parent or family member of a child with CD or an educator who teaches students with CD, you might be wondering why you should care about the educational success of students with CD. Allow me to make a case for why the effective education of this special group of students should be at the top of everyone's radar.

First and foremost, being an educated adult is necessary for basic independent functioning in today's society. One cannot care for himself if he does not possess the abilities to responsibly navigate the kind of day-to-day tasks and decisions that most adults thoughtlessly engage in and consider to be routine. We must ask what happens when adults are not functional, that is, when they cannot perform these basic functions for themselves. Well, while their parents or caretakers are alive, people with CD depend heavily on them, relying on their caretakers to navigate their lives for them, make decisions for them, care for their basic shelter, food and personal care needs, and ensure their overall health, safety and well-being. However, what happens when their caretakers either pass away or reach a stage of life where they can no longer take care of their CD dependent? You guessed it: they become the responsibility of society.

At this point, your tax dollars go to subsidize the functioning of adults with CD who cannot care for themselves because they do not possess a high enough level of mental functioning to do so. Thus, it is often the case when the primary caregiver of a person with CD passes away (or in some cases, walks away) that an individual with CD becomes a dependent of the state. Who pays for their care? You do... or at least your tax dollars do.

There are two major federal programs that the U.S. government uses to provide financial assistance to people who have disabilities. The first program, Social Security Disability Insurance (SSDI) is a program that provides earnings to individuals who have worked and paid Social Security taxes for at least 40 quarters after they become disabled and are unable to continue working. The more they've paid into the Social Security system, the higher the financial assistance they receive from the government. The second program is the Supplemental Security Income (SSI) program, which provides financial assistance to people who have little to no work history, low income, and few resources to sustain them. Considered to be a traditional welfare program, this average current benefit paid out to single individuals who qualify is $735 a month. Although this monthly check is automatically supplemented with Medicaid in most states, these combined benefits alone are hardly enough to support a sustainable lifestyle.[14] Nevertheless, when adults with cognitive disabilities are unable to care for themselves, we as taxpayers will inevitably end up footing the bill. When you multiply the nearly 6.5 million people in the U.S. who have an intellectual disability by the $735 a month plus Medicaid expenses, we're talking about billions of tax dollars spent to support these individuals who are not sufficiently equipped to support themselves.

If the "help students with CD now or pay with your tax dollars later" line of reasoning doesn't convince you to want to help students with CD, let me try another approach. Allow me to appeal to the basic human value of caring about the well-being of all people, regardless of difference. Empathy. I'm relying on your sensitivity to the documented fact that the current educational and life outcomes of cognitively impaired individuals are significantly lower than the outcomes of non-impaired individuals, and I'm trusting that you will not think this is fair, especially because it's a problem that can be fixed.

Are you aware that people with cognitive disabilities are at a significantly increased risk of being homeless?[15] Perhaps you weren't aware that landlords will often deny individuals with CD the opportunity to rent housing because individuals with CD tend to have speech, odd behaviors, and an overall way of functioning that are hard to understand. Then, if landlords do allow individuals with CD to rent housing, it is often lost. "People with cognitive impairments who do obtain housing often lose it through eviction, because these impairments leave them unable to figure out how to pay for rent and utilities, or how to maintain residences appropriately."[16]

Here's another thing. Did you know that 35% of people with cognitive disabilities live below the poverty line? In 2018, the mean earnings of individuals with cognitive disabilities was $23,000. Studies have consistently produced findings linking intellectual disability to poverty, indicating that people with cognitive disabilities are significantly more likely to live in poverty than people who do not have cognitive disabilities. The primary reason for this is lack of access to income-earning opportunities. Research indicates that "job training programs for people with intellectual disabilities have historically targeted low-pay-ing, part-time, entry level jobs offering few benefits or opportu-nities for promotion or advancement."[17] A study in which proj-ect managers and human resource professionals were surveyed about their perceptions regarding hiring people with disabilities revealed that they had negative perceptions about this popula-tion's ability to be productive, psychologically adjust to the work environment, operate with social maturity, and demonstrate interpersonal skills, leading to a reduced likelihood of extend-ing candidates with CD a job offer.[18] We must understand that it's not that individuals with cognitive disabilities don't want to work. According to The American Association of People with Disabilities, "two-thirds of people with disabilities are of work-ing age and want to work."[19] Unfortunately, the stigma that fol-lows their lives marginalizes them to the outskirts of the work-force and relegates them to a life of poverty.

The cascade effect that living below the poverty line has on the lives of individuals with CD is also a matter of concern. For ex-ample, adults who have cognitive disabilities are disadvantaged across every marker of health inequality, a direct result of the reduced employment opportunities and low incomes to which they are typically relegated as a result of their disability.[20] The environmental risks that go hand-in-hand with living in poverty can further increase the likelihood of people with cognitive dis-abilities living in poor health.

One of the things that makes us human is an innate desire to ensure that everyone is okay, that every human has a fair chance at life. Well, people with CD were born with the chips stacked against them, and they deserve our empathy. They were at a crit-ical disadvantage from the moment they entered the world, and nothing has been fair for them ever since. However, this does not have to remain their lot in life. By offering them a different kind of education, one that integrates AI into their instructional cycle and overall functioning, we might not be able to level the playing field for them, but we can at least come close. Special education that leans on AI to augment the learning of students with CD can bring them close to functioning in such a way that they have a fair chance at getting as close to living an independent life as possible.

I know that there will always be people who oppose our efforts and who will never think it's okay to give students with CD extra considerations and advantages in the classroom. I'm a realist, so I know that these detractors will always be there, regardless of the strength of the logical arguments I raise or of the number of passionate appeals to their humanity I make. However, what I am promoting does not require 100% of everyone to be on board; it just requires that a critical, collective mass of empathetic individuals stand up with me to advocate for the needs of those who cannot advocate for themselves. If we do not all stand together to present an innovative solution to improving the educational outcomes, and subsequently, the post-educational lives of individuals with cognitive disabilities, it's not just the CD population that will pay the cost; we will all pay the cost, because inequity is a cost that is ultimately shared by everyone. When you balance things out by operating from a position of equity (I'll talk more about this later), everyone benefits.

We clearly have a group that is underperforming and underearning in society. The good news is that it's a fixable problem. If we could only have the empathy, compassion, and courage to do what is necessary to improve their performance and earnings and help them become contributing members of society, we would all win. All it takes is giving them access to innovative learning opportunities they've never had before.

Special Education Pedagogy:
Outdated in Disruption & Innovation

It is no secret to anyone in education that special education has not changed its approaches over the past 25 years. Nearly all of the practices that we use in the classroom today to provide learning for these students are the same practices that we were using in the 1990s. When we consider this reality, it's no wonder that special education pedagogy produces high school graduates that fail to meet competencies necessary to live as functional, independent adults after graduation. The world, which is making innovations at the speed of thought, is changing day by day, and our approaches to special education are left behind as ancient relics of the past.

The problem is not a love for the students or a lack of passion in the teachers. The teachers are passionate. However, the wrong approach done passionately will still fail to yield the necessary results. The problem is the outdated practices that we continue to use to educate students with cognitive deficiencies, even though they have been yielding poor educational and post-educational outcomes for decades. A grand innovation of the special education pedagogy must occur if we desire to see different outcomes in the future. To do nothing – to maintain the status quo – is to say that we are fine with the way that things are. However, I'm convinced that no one can look at the current outcomes that we produce for these students and be fine with them. At least, no one with a heart.

It's my belief that, in general, there's a lot more that we can do to help individuals with cognitive disabilities. However, how we can serve this community better is not something that most people spend any time thinking about, especially if no one with a cognitive disability occupies their immediate life space. In fact, we largely ignore the CD community and take for granted that the way things are is the way things have to be. I don't consider this to be true. I uphold the position that not only should a lot more be done for individuals with CD, but a lot more can be done to help those in this community. The existing condition of special education is not inalterable; significant advancements can be made if we reject the status quo and make the decision to invest our time, energy and resources into a collective change effort.

Someone recently asked me if I thought that the reason that those working in special education continue to operate the same way they've operated for decades because they feel there's nothing more they can do, or because they feel defeated. My response was that I don't think that special education workers are defeated. I think they are committed and passionate and that they do everything in their power to improve the lives of children with cognitive disabilities. However, while I applaud the passion and commitment of our nation's special education workers, these are not enough to ensure that students with CD graduate from high school with the level of intelligence necessary to take care of themselves. If you, as a special education worker, have made little difference in the outcomes of students with CD over the past 25 years, it's not your individual efforts that are the problem. It's your approach. The wrong approach taken passionately is not going to produce the outcomes that are desired, regardless of how committed and hardworking you are. It's my belief that we need to introduce a new approach to special education workers so that we can make greater gains in the education of students with CD. We need to engage some fresh, innovative thinking in order to produce some different outcomes.

JACKIE'S STORY

Jackie loves going to school and engaging with her friends. Jackie, however, has a cognitive disability and has difficulty writing. Jackie is mainstreamed in a regular education classroom. During a class writing assignment, Ms. Singleton, the special education teacher, often takes Jackie and four other special education students aside, working with them in small groups to complete writing assignments. This pulls Jackie away from her friends, and she would rather stay integrated with them than be pulled apart from them in class. Seeing that Jackie gets a little down and embarrassed when she's pulled to the back of the room with the other special education students, Ms. Singleton provides Jackie with an alternative. She tells Jackie that for the next assignment, instead of having to leave her peers as she completes assignments, Jackie could remain at her desk and write alongside her friends using a tablet or laptop. Jackie loved this idea and now uses this technology to complete her writing assignments. Occasionally, Jackie asks for Ms. Singleton's help, but most of the time, Jackie turns to her classmates for help. At the completion of the writing assignments, Jackie uses her tablet to read her work back to her aloud while she listens to it through earphones. Both her confidence and her grades have significantly improved in the class since she began using technology.

This is the power of AI in education.

INNOVATION CURVE:

The Opportunity for Education to Position Itself at the Forefront of AI Development

Ever hear of the cliché "A day late and a dollar short?" That's what comes to mind when I think of education's relationship with innovation. Innovation happens every day, in every nation, in ways that can affect every industry and every individual around the world in some way. So much is happening with innovation! You go to bed, wake up, and there's a new technology, process or product on the market that has pushed the limits of what already existed in that space. This new innovation will do things faster, allow consumers to produce more with fewer resources, and produce outcomes significantly better than their current outcomes. In an instant, the "old thing" has to give place to the "new thing" that has disrupted the market, and the "old thing" is rendered obsolete.

When industries, companies, organizations, and individuals hear about all of the new tools and resources that are developed through strategic innovation, they rush to adopt the innovative approach. They want to work more efficiently, perform optimally, and achieve better results with this new innovation, so they jump on it – fast! These are called "early adopters." As soon as a new innovation becomes available that promises to produce their desired outcomes in a better way, they adopt it. Then, there are "laggards." These are the ones that see the new innovation but want to stand back for a while and watch to see how it fares. Rather than integrating what is faster, more cost-effective, and able to help them achieve better outcomes, they say, "Things are okay the way they are, so we'll stick to what we're already using." While everyone else is benefitting from the new innovation, these laggards lag behind everyone else. Over time, after the innovation becomes a normal part of the marketplace, and lots of people have adopted it, the laggards eventually come aboard and adopt the no-longer-new technology.

The education industry has historically fallen into the laggard category, consistently falling on the back end of innovation. Innovation has not traditionally been a value of education; it has seemed to be more comfortable with sticking to the status quo in terms of how it does things. Yes, the industry keeps the instructional content updated by ensuring that textbooks have the most up-to-date information, but in terms of pedagogy, things are different. There is a structural inertia in the education industry that tends to keep it stuck in the "this is the way we do things" mode, and this is to the detriment of the industry.

There are two challenges with the education industry occupying the laggard space relative to innovation. First, the education industry needs to undergo constant change just like other industries that relate to innovation as early adopters in order to remain relevant and efficient in the service it offers: learning outcomes. Without constant innovation – updates that will improve performance and outcomes – it stands to produce poorer outcomes than it has the potential to produce. Second, education's laggard relationship with the most innovative industries, like technology, results in a perception that it is not interested in a close relationship with innovation, or that it does not maintain a strong value for what innovation offers. Consequently, when technology developers are creating new technologies, they rarely do so with the education industry in mind. This means that education is at the back of the innovation curve where new things rarely happen. This is problematic.

The Plight of the Education Industry: Ignored in Innovation and Always Behind the Development Curve

Education's historical relationship with the technology industry is one that must be addressed. Although it has not had a close relationship with technology in the past, this is something that can change. However, it is only in first acknowledging that the education industry has traditionally remained at the back of the innovation curve that we can take the necessary steps to try to position it at the front of the innovation curve where amazing things happen and potential is unlimited.

In the next 10 years, AI technology is going to touch every field of every industry that exists. The thing is, conversations about the mind-blowing, innovative ways in which this technology will be used in various industries are happening *today*. Right now, technology industry leaders are planning for what our future will look like decades down the line. They are sitting around tables in conference rooms, making diagrams on whiteboards, and strategizing about what they envision, what accommodations need to be made, what data needs to be collected, and what structures need to be put into place now so that the world can benefit later. They're looking at how AI can be used in the medical industry to provide precise speed-of-light access to medical knowledge and to platforms on which patient diagnosis and treatment can occur without any human interaction. They're discussing how AI can be used in aeronautics to navigate the controls of an aircraft as it makes a transatlantic flight without the presence of humans in the cockpit. They're tossing around ideas about how AI can be used in the auto industry to remotely fix a car at its owner's home without having to bring the car to a repair shop. The list of the potentials that AI technology industry pioneers is dreaming up is limitless.

Here's the problem: rarely, if ever, is education at the forefront of these industry conversations. Most innovation is developed without the education industry and its specific needs in mind. Instead, innovation is traditionally developed with other more "valuable" industries in mind and then eventually retrofitted to "less-valuable" industries like education. As a result, when technology developers are looking at the vast potentials of how AI innovations can impact industries, your child's elementary, middle and high school are likely never to appear on their radar.

Some people might not see retrofitting technology to education as a big deal. They might ask, "Who cares if education is at the front end of development? As long as innovations can be applied to the education industry later on down the road, isn't that all that matters?" The easy answer to this question is "No." There are challenges to retrofitting that make it an undesirable option. Consider the following:

1. **Retrofitting is expensive.** A lot of additional time and energy has to be invested into making a thing fit (or work for) something it was not originally designed to fit.

2. **Retrofitting is inconvenient.** It can be a frustrating process, because it requires taking something that was made for industry A and making it work for industry B, especially considering that these are two completely different industries.

3. **Retrofitting results in compromised effectiveness.** When trying to take something made for one industry and using it for another, two industries that are altogether different in their systems, structures, processes, values, approaches – everything – there will inevitably be a lack of alignment between the two. The retrofitted innovation may never fit the second industry perfectly, resulting in that industry using the new tool or resource from a compromised position.

4. **Retrofitting creates performance gaps**. When applied to the industry for which it was originally created, an innovation can perform at 100%. However, when retrofitted to a new industry, there is a low likelihood that the new industry will realize the same high performance, because the inner workings of the innovation were not developed to help it achieve these performance levels.

Why the Disregard of the Education Industry by Companies Driving Innovation?

Part of me understands why education is traditionally ignored in innovation; it's not exactly on the top of the list of money-making industries, and technology is typically driven by the dollar. The other part of me believes that education should be at the top of the list when technology developers are seeking to improve how things are done. Educating children might not produce tons of revenue, but an investment in them is an investment in our future. One day, we'll have to pass the torch to them to lead the way, and when we do, we want to ensure that we are putting our nation in the best and most prepared hands possible. What good would it do to advance our society leaps and bounds through technology and then hand things over to a group of graduates ill-prepared to maintain the progress that was made? I might be biased because I'm a professional educator, but I strongly believe that conversations about how technology innovations can augment or improve the way we do things should always include the diverse and changing needs of education.

Some will try to point the finger at the education industry. "It's their own fault! Why don't educators bring their technology ideas to technology leaders? Why not stand up for their industry and demand to have a voice at the table where innovations in technology are discussed?" they ask. I don't ask such questions, because I don't fault educators for being ignored in critical conversations about technology. They don't have time for such tasks. Think about it. Educators are not experts in technology. Every day, these often overworked, underpaid, and underappreciated dedicated professionals have their hands full and their attention squarely focused on dealing with children who need their help *now*. That's their priority, as it should be. In light of this, it would be hard for them to work out concepts and strategies that combine the two fields. Nonetheless, I desire to put an end to the habit of the education industry being habitually dismissed and disregarded as a serious potential recipient of the technology innovations that are moving other industries forward. In fact, this was my main impetus for undertaking this project.

A Unique Opportunity to Shift Education to the Forefront of Conversations in AI Development

Today, the education industry is in a unique position to emerge to the forefront of the innovation curve in AI development. However, it is not a move that can take place until the education industry dares to break free of structural inertia holding it in the past and embrace the opportunity to shape AI innovation.

According to AI expert Katrina Wakefield of SAS (Statistical Analysis Systems):

> Organizations that respond rapidly to opportunities in artificial intelligence application will have the advantage in the landscape of the future. But, because AI is evolving rapidly, the challenge is to ensure that the business has the necessary strategies and plans to support AI capabilities as they become available, and the right technical infrastructure to support AI implementation. For many businesses, it's not a question of "if" but rather "when" to adopt AI. On that basis, monitoring the development of AI technology and planning far in advance is necessary to adopt AI successfully.[21]

Unless the education industry responds rapidly to the opportunities that AI offers to our future, we will lose any advantage we could ever have in being a central part of the development of AI solutions that could benefit our schools, specifically our special education classrooms. Instead of waiting for the industry to fully develop its core processes without education in mind, we must ensure that we are at the development table, taking part in the development conversations about the infrastructure of AI applications that stand to significantly improve the outcomes of our students. Otherwise, we position ourselves to merely be retrofitted with systems that were not developed with the needs of our students in mind.

AI is something that will inevitably be integrated into our schools. As Wakefield put it, "It's not a question of 'if' but rather 'when' to adopt AI." We must begin preparing for it now. We must build an infrastructure in our schools that stands ready to adopt and support the implementation of AI. It is my hope that once AI is integrated into our systems, because we will have played a role in its development from the inception stage, we will be sufficiently prepared to run with it – a perfect fit between the problems that we have and the solutions it provides.

The Outer Limits of Cognition: Why AI Developers Should Center Technology Development on the CD Community

There's a really good reason that AI developers should center their AI development efforts on students with CD. Individuals with cognitive disabilities represent the outer limits of what AI exists to do: mimic the cognitive functions of the human mind. If AI pioneers begin to systematically tackle the narrow real-world challenges of individuals with CD, these hardest-case scenarios offer amazing opportunities to gather data. AI specifically developed for CD has the opportunity to change the popular public narrative of AI as "killer robot" to AI for social good that benefits everyone.

Here's the principle that I'm attempting to promote: Cognitive disabilities, particularly in the development of AI, are a valuable source of untapped inspiration and provide ample opportunity to drive technological development. In the medical field, advancements benefitting general medicine often come from developments made to cure specific diseases. The opportunity to drive AI development is no different; advancements benefitting the general world of AI can come from developments made from using AI specifically to increase the learning outcomes of individuals with CD.

Using AI to solve the complex challenges of individuals with CD also boosts the level of the AI development and technology that will ultimately be available for everyone else's consumption in the general population. When developers accept the challenge of centering their next level of development around tackling the solving of a problem that individuals with CD encounter on a daily basis, they have the opportunity to factor into any AI prototype development the capacity to handle some of the most demanding cognitive challenges humans encounter. Necessity is the mother of invention, and individuals with CD have myriad needs that can both inspire and drive the innovative development of AI-based technological solutions.

Individuals with CD offer a wide range of moderate to severe challenges, which AI has the potential to resolve. For example, consider that individuals with CD may also have neurological speech impairments. For these individuals, it can be extremely difficult to express themselves or for other individuals to understand their speech. To solve this problem, Google's Project Euphonia team, which is part of the AI for Social Good program, has been developing AI to improve the ability of computers to understand diverse speech patterns. Google's AI for Social Good program focuses Google's AI expertise on solving humanitarian and environmental challenges by "applying core Google research and engineering efforts to projects with positive societal impact, including partnering with experts, and empowering the ecosystem with tools and resources..."[22]

Google has partnered with ALS Therapy Development Institute and the ALS Residence Initiative to record voices of individuals who have ALS (Amyotrophic lateral sclerosis), a progressive neuro-degenerative disease that affects nerve cells in the brain and spinal cord. With ALS, an individual may lose the ability to speak, eat, move and breathe. One of the goals of Google's work in this area is to use AI to train computers to better recognize less-common types of speech, such as speech from someone who has a speech impairment, and then allow a computer to reliably transcribe that speech. After a computer accurately recognizes the speech of an individual, he or she has access to all of the functions available on the computer.

In addition to improving speech recognition for individuals who have speech impairments, Google is also training AI systems to detect sounds or gestures and then take actions such as generating spoken commands for Google Home and other programs available on the computer. Google believes that this research can be applied to larger groups of people and to different speech impairments.[23] Once this technology is perfected, imagine being able to control your computer through gestures! The possibilities are endless. This is yet another example of how meeting the needs of the disability community through AI technology development may ultimately provide benefit to everyone.

In the automotive world, Formula 1 racing has driven the technological advancements of the gasoline engine. Formula E, the all-electric version of Formula 1, is driving the technological advancements of electric engines that find their way into the electric cars that are available at local car dealerships for everyday driving by those in the general population. The challenges NASA solves in order to effectively operate in space translates into the development of over 1,600 new technologies each year. Thousands of those products, services and processes transfer to spur innovation and growth in the consumer marketplace. In very simple terms, it's all about centering the development of technology on the most extreme cases possible, the outer limits of potential scenarios, so that technology is inherently designed to work with the most extreme of cases and still produce the most optimal results. If they can make the technology work for these cases, it will automatically be able to work for everyone else, including the moderate cases, the category where most of the population typically falls.

If technology developers continue to develop AI technology without the most extreme cases of those who live with deficits in cognition, their innovations will be impotent when applied to this population. Sure, they can go back and try to adjust what they have developed to accommodate these hard cases, but because this population is an afterthought, it will never work on people with CD as effectively as it could have if the technology was developed with this specific population's needs in mind. In the most extreme cases – people with severe cognitive disabilities – there is a strong possibility that the technology will not work at all. Thus, innovating AI technology without using individuals with CD as test cases during the development will result in the creation of technology that will never be as powerful as it could have been. It will also result in products that are expensive to make work, inconvenient to use, ineffective at solving the problem and that provide only marginal performance when they actually do work at all. We must advocate for the population of individuals with CD to be at the center of development rather than just an afterthought. If we embrace this mission, we have the opportunity to push innovation and creativity to the edges of human experience, resulting in the development of technologies that ultimately benefit everyone – individuals with and without CD – at a greater level.

There's also a hidden potential benefit in using the CD population as test cases for the development of AI: if the cognitive disability population becomes the center of AI development, the disability might begin to be perceived as a benefit, removing some of the negative connotation that surrounds these unique individuals. This is a great opportunity for the technology industry to not only develop AI technology with the power to solve the needs of subjects with the greatest level of complexity but to help remove the stigma associated with cognitive disabilities.

JENNIFER'S STORY

Jennifer reads at a third-grade reading level, although she is currently in the 6th grade and attends class with other 6th graders. She has made many friends in her 6th grade class and talks with them all the time, sharing stories, laughing, and having fun. Mrs. Spontiff, Jennifer's reading teacher, has noticed that during reading, Jennifer is almost like a different child. Instead of being bubbly and engaging, Jennifer becomes quiet and disengages. When Mrs. Spontiff asks Jennifer about how she feels about reading class, Jennifer says she feels "stupid" because she cannot read as well as the other students. Mrs. Spontiff tells Jennifer that she is not stupid and that she would like Jennifer to try using a text-to-speech program for the class reading assignments. Mrs. Spontiff tells Jennifer that during reading assignments, she can use the classroom computer, a laptop, or a cellphone and use Microsoft Word to read the assignment aloud to her as she listens to it through earphones. Jennifer was skeptical about doing this at first, but after a couple of tries, she finds the process easy to manage. Now, Jennifer is voluntarily and enthusiastically contributing to classroom discussions about the reading material along with her friends. While Jennifer's reading is only at a third-grade level, she can listen to sixth-grade reading level content. Jennifer's exposure to and engagement with sixth-grade reading level content allows Jennifer to keep up with her classmates. She couldn't be more pleased!

**This is the power of
AI in education.**

CHEATER

Conventional vs. Artificial Intelligence

I confessed in the Introduction at the beginning of this book that I don't have all of the answers about artificial intelligence, especially regarding its use among individuals with cognitive disabilities. In fact, I admitted to quite the opposite: I have a lot of questions about the matter. My goal is to begin the conversation about the intersections between AI and CD so that students in special needs classrooms around the nation can begin benefitting from the amazing benefits that AI technology offers. However, we'll never be able to reach this point without asking some important questions and taking time to thoughtfully consider how they can be answered in a non-traditional, out-of-the-box manner.

My own questioning began back when I was in graduate school, working on my master's degree in special education and it extended into my doctoral work. My doctoral dissertation topic was about how to create a framework for knowledge management in special education, and this project is an extension of that research. Organizational and Business knowledge management theory examines how people, information and technology work together to support business goals. Although the theory is typically used in research on business organizations, its application is directly relevant to education, because we need to do a better job of managing the knowledge in our education organizations.

In my dissertation, I asked myself the question, "If there was a framework for managing knowledge within an education organization, what would it look like?" I knew that things would begin with the teachers, because they are the knowledge engine of the school; if you go into a school without teachers present, nothing will get done. However, for all of the teachers to have knowledge is not enough; if the knowledge they possess is not managed, everyone else in the organization will miss out on the benefit of what they know. For example, let's say that someone has worked in a position at a school for years, and then she retires, and the school goes out and hires another teacher to take her place. That new teacher will not be able to do the job as well as the previous teacher, because the previous teacher did so much more than the basics – well beyond what was on the job description that the new teacher received. The question is, how do you capture all of that "extra" information that teachers have in the school so that you can extend it to other people in the organization? This is a quintessential knowledge management question!

Now, let me take things a step further. We know that knowledge management is a relevant discussion for an education organization – or any organization for that matter – but what about its relevance to discussions about how we as individuals manage knowledge?

Think about it. In a school, a lot of different teachers possess a lot of different knowledge, and if the organization is going to be all the richer for the knowledge these teachers possess, the organization is going to have to find a way (typically through technology) to gain access to all of this knowledge, organize the knowledge, store the knowledge, and leverage the knowledge for the collective benefit of the organization when necessary.

Can this argument not also pertain to individual knowledge management? Let's consider this question from the individual perspective of a special education student. There's a lot of information out there that he needs to access. If he's going to be all the richer for knowing this information, he's going to have to find a way (let's go ahead and say through technology) to gain access to all this knowledge, organize the knowledge, store the knowledge, and leverage the knowledge for his benefit when necessary. When we look at things this way, the translation of knowledge management theory from organization to individual seems like a reasonable one, doesn't it?

Currently, we expect students to manage their own knowledge in the classroom. It's up to them to collect, or access, all of the information their teacher and textbooks are teaching, organize it in their minds and in their notes, store it in their brain, and leverage the knowledge to answer test questions when the time comes. The more effectively they manage their knowledge, the more academically successful they will be in the classroom. However, what about students who do not have the capacity to manage their own knowledge? Why can't we manage the knowledge for them? Can we develop a way to help them with the process of knowledge management in order to be academically successful? I say we can!

When technology is discussed in the context of knowledge management in organizations, it is discussed as a tool to be used in the process of gathering, organizing, storing, and leveraging information. However, that's not how I propose it to be used in helping special education students to gather, organize, store, and leverage information. What I'm proposing is that technology becomes more than just a supplemental tool for them. I propose that technology becomes an extension of their brain, that they depend on technology so heavily to augment their brain that it becomes a part of who they are.

In the same way that people without their own hands use prosthetic hands as natural extensions of their bodies to function and facilitate life in as close to a normal fashion as everyone else, I want to see people with cognitive disabilities to use AI technology as a natural extension of their mental functioning and facilitate life in as close to a normal fashion as everyone else. We are more than happy to see people with physical disabilities compensate for a body part they are missing, and we do not criticize their total dependence on whatever tool is necessary for them to counteract their physical deficiency. In the same way, I am advocating for us being equally supportive of students with CD developing a total dependence on AI as a tool that will counteract their mental deficiency.

> I want the use of AI technology among students with CD to become so prevalent that it becomes a normalized part of their daily functioning.

I want the use of AI technology among students with CD to become so prevalent that it becomes a normalized part of their daily functioning. I want the way they access technology and access their brain to become so interchangeable that there is no longer a distinction between how and if they've used one or the other. I want technology to become how students with CD "know" the knowledge that they do not possess in their own brain.

This brings another question to the forefront of the conversation: What does it mean to "know" or to "learn" something? Really think about this before you answer the question, or else you'll answer it based on learned tradition. As you ponder this, allow me to challenge your traditional, classical understanding of what it means to "know." I think you'll find that the concept you've been holding onto about what it means to "know" and "learn" is more a result of what you've been taught through conditioning rather than a result of thoughtful, deliberate reasoning about the matter.

Conventional Definitions of "Knowledge"

Theories about knowledge, or what it means to "know" or "learn," go as far back as the days in which philosophical greats like Plato and Aristotle lived. Plato asserted that knowledge is "justified true belief," or "true opinion combined with reason," also known as the "classical definition of knowledge."[24] According to Socrates, knowledge is "absolute truth." According to Merriam-Webster, knowledge is "the fact or condition of knowing something with familiarity gained through experience or association" or "the body of truth, information, and principles acquired by humankind."[25] Definitions of what it means to "know" abound.

The Calculator:
A Historical Example of How Biases
About What It Means to "Know" Fumbled
Technology Implementation

The work of education is all about extending the learning of the student or helping the student to know. The primary indicator that learning has occurred is that a student knows more than he/she did before receiving instruction of some sort. However, does a student's learning or acquisition of knowledge have to be centered on what that student knows in his own mind? If a student can access knowledge from an external source, thus providing him with more knowledge than he had before, is this truly learning? If you say it's not, ask yourself, "Why not?" Here's another question: Do you believe that accessing technology to "know" the answer to a question is any less "learning" than accessing one's own mind to "know" the answer to a question? The way you answer these questions will ultimately determine whether you'll embrace the use of AI in special education classrooms to produce better quality learning outcomes for students with CD.

Before you consider your answers to these questions, it may be helpful to explore the historical context in which calculators have been used by students with and without CD over the past decades. All of the main themes related to the use of AI that I explore in this book have been related to calculators. Why? Because when calculators were introduced in the mid-1970s, they were considered a new, intimidating and controversial technology to educators, much like AI is regarded today. Thus, an examination of the calculator's adaptation in education is a necessary one for gaining a better understanding of the proposed adaption of AI in classroom learning, especially as it pertains to extending the learning of the student outside of the student's own intrinsic cognitive abilities.

The debate surrounding the controversial use of calculators in U.S. classrooms has spanned decades. The calculator controversy in mathematics education pits those who believe calculators act as a crutch that limits students' skill development against those who believe calculators serve as a tool to augment learning for students who have already developed a conceptual understanding of mathematical concepts.[26]

Critics base their contentions about calculator use in the classroom on the ideas that calculators reduce students' motivation to master basic mathematical facts, decrease students' ability to identify errors, and make them dependent on the tool.[27] Their resistance to this supplemental tool is documented. A 1982 report indicated that there was a widespread public concern over the use of calculators by children who had not mastered the traditional pencil-and-paper methods of computation,[28] while a decade later, a 1992 study found that various members of the society had strong reservations about the educational use of calculators, often reflecting their own experience of learning mathematics without access to technology.[29]

Among the camp of critics who resist the use of technology in the classroom are teachers. Although the integration of all types of technology into the classroom is viewed as an effective instructional strategy for improving student learning, many teachers often do not have favorable attitudes towards the effectiveness of technology. While teachers' attitudes about technology in the classroom might seem insignificant, they are not; they impact the rate of adaptation, the extent to which technologies are used, and how adequately they are integrated into the learning process. Research indicates that one of the primary reasons technology was historically not engaged at a more widespread level as an instructional tool in classrooms was due to the influence of teachers' attitudes towards technologies and their ability to use them effectively.[30]

Educators' attitudes matter because they influence, to a great degree, how effectively technology is integrated into classroom learning, thus having a significant impact on classroom adaptation of technology. Their attitudes, therefore, should not be dismissed. For example, teachers who are not proficient with modern technologies tend to employ methods that encourage rote memorization of facts rather than learner-centered approaches intended to provide students with learning mathematics through relational understanding. Their apprehension with the use of technology: technology use inhibits students' basic computational skills. One research study showed that 73% of teachers in the sample wanted students to memorize the multiplication tables and learn pencil-and-paper arithmetic before using calculators because they could hamper the learning of basic facts.[31] Other teachers have been reluctant to integrate the use of calculators in the classroom because they feared it would contribute to lack of mathematical understanding and threaten students' basic skill development.[32]

The challenge with these teachers' positions is that they are based on the teachers' own experiences, attitudes, beliefs, past practices and personal theories of knowledge rather than on the research.[33] There is no shortage of scientific research studies that have analyzed the effects of calculator use in the classroom and discovered results that directly counter teachers' beliefs that technology contributes to lack of mathematical understanding and threatens students' basic computational skills development. Thus, their resistant attitudes towards calculator use, as powerfully ingrained as they are, are largely unsubstantiated.

Proponents of calculator use in the classroom, on the other hand, typically rely on research science and the endorsements of professional organizations that have taken a deep dive into the data to validate their acceptance of this type of technology being integrated into student learning. For example, in a meta-analysis of research on the impact of calculators on student achievement and attitude, researchers found that students' problem-solving skills improved with calculator use with no harm in skill development, even with repeated calculator use.[34] Also, the National Council of Teachers of Mathematics endorses appropriate calculator use in mathematics education (i.e., to enhance students' mathematics understanding).[35] Throughout research, calculators, as assistive technology, have been shown to support not only students' correct performance in mathematics, but also their efficiency in solving mathematical problems.[36]

Shortly after its introduction into the classroom, researchers began studying the effects of calculator use on students' conceptual development and computational skills. Research results showed that calculators could foster conceptual development, reduce computational errors, and reduce students' fears of mathematics.[37] Researchers from another study found that calculators could assist students in solving problems with real-world data and allow students a more efficient means to try strategies for problem solving.[38]

Further, the grade level at which calculators are introduced into student learning does not diminish the overwhelming body of research evidence suggesting that calculator use is safe and effective. Most studies suggest that introduction of calculators as early as preschool does not harm computational ability. To the contrary, these studies affirm that appropriate use of calculators enhances young children's ability to learn basic facts and that students who use calculators frequently exhibit more advanced concept development and problem solving skills than those who do not use calculators.[39]

Another variable that researchers have factored into their studies, cognitive disability, has produced research results surrounding the use of calculators in student learning that are consistent with results of studies using students who do not have CD. Calculators are, today, the most widely-used accommodation for students with disabilities.[40] Overall, research has shown that calculators can serve as a cognitive prosthesis and augment mathematical performance of students with disabilities.[41]

For example, in a study comparing the use of calculators and the paper-and-pencil method for solving subtraction problems with junior high school students with mild intellectual disability, students improved performance and accuracy in solving subtraction problems with the use of calculators.[42] The positive impact of a calculator was particularly noticeable with regards to students' responses to word problems. The students did better with a calculator than without one, and when given a calculator, these students performed similarly to their peers without disabilities in solving problems.[43]

Despite decades of past research providing support for the use of calculators in mathematical learning among both students with and without intellectual disabilities, negative attitudes, perceptions and beliefs surrounding the use of this technology in the classroom triumphed in the end. As a result, today, calculators are not fully implemented in classrooms for use as cognitive prostheses that can augment mathematical performance among students with CD. Educators, giving in to subjective assumptions, fears of the unknown and personal bias, influenced the adaptation of calculator use, fumbling the ball on fully integrating this beneficial technology into student learning. Ultimately, students were the victims of their unsubstantiated attitudes, being deprived of a chance to experience greater learning outcomes through experiencing all that technology has to offer.

However, we have a unique opportunity for a do-over as we propose the introduction of AI technology into the classroom to augment student learning. Just as calculators were a new technology trying to make their way into the classroom in the 1970s, AI is a new technology trying to make its way into the classroom today. Educator attitudes sabotaged the full implementation of calculators then. Let's not allow the same to happen now. This time let's give greater weight to the scientific research than to assumptions, fears, and personal bias. This time, let's put the needs of the students ahead of our own resistance to learning, understanding, and integrating the use of modern technology into augmenting the educational process. Let's pledge to learn from our past mistakes and not lose the opportunity AI presents to today's learners with intellectual disabilities.

Is "Knowing" Through the Use of Artificial Intelligence in School Really Cheating?

We must rethink how and under what circumstances technology should be used in the classroom – without calling it "cheating." AI can help students with CD by helping them access what they need to "know" in order to arrive at the right answers. AI would not be a replacement for their brainpower; it would be an augmentation of their cognition, compensating for their cognitive shortcomings. If students with CD could use technology to access the things they need to "know," then by definition, they would still be "learning." By the time they graduated from high school, their learning outcomes would be so much more advanced than their special education predecessors who graduated without the privilege of augmenting their learning with AI technology.

"But isn't it cheating to just give these special education students the answer?" people will ask. To me, this whole notion is the equivalent of individuals with physical disabilities needing a wheelchair and people telling them to get up out of their wheelchairs and walk at a normal pace. They look at the people in wonder and disbelief and reply, "We'd love to, but we CAN'T!" In the conversation surrounding students with CD using AI technology in the classroom, the AI would be the wheelchair. Believe me, they would give everything they own to be able to cognitively function like and keep pace with the rest of society; they are just physically unable to do so because of their cognitive shortcomings. Without assistance, they will never be able to function at the same level as the average person in society. Thus, it is our moral responsibility to put into place the aids and supports to compensate for what they need to function as "normally" as possible, just as we do for those who are disabled by physical mobility issues.

A Brief History of Artificial Intelligence

Although I have been working in education for more than two decades, I have always possessed a passion for technology. About 10 years ago, when the limitless potentials of AI began to be discussed, I couldn't help but take notice. Technology innovators began to see AI as the holy grail of the industry: the first to develop a computer or machine that could think like a human, mimicking human cognition, or intelligence, to a T, would be declared the winner of the biggest prize in history. However, as they all began racing towards this grand prize, I began to think about how we have a whole section of society that needs help with cognition: the community of more than 16 million people in the U.S. living with cognitive disabilities.[44] The potentials of how AI could benefit those whose greatest fundamental need in life was something to compensate for their lack of intelligence due to cognitive shortcomings excited me, and I have been a passionate follower of the industry ever since.

Just in case you're totally unfamiliar with AI, allow me to give you a primer of the background and potential that lies within this branch of technology.

Decades ago, in 1943, scientists Warren McCulloch and logician Walter Pitts developed the first piece of AI, called the "artificial neuron."[45] Since that time, scientists, mathematicians and engineers began touting AI to be the "next big thing" in technology. However, the practical uses of AI in various industries actually didn't begin until the 2000s, which is when I began to take notice of it.[46]

While most people think of AI as one monolithic technology, it is actually an umbrella term under which several different technologies reside, including:[47]

- Machine learning
- Deep learning
- Robotics
- Computer vision
- Cognitive computing
- Artificial general intelligence
- Natural language processing
- Knowledge reasoning

Each of these technologies reside at different levels of AI, as AI is not a one-size-fits-all space. For example, on a consumer level of AI, we have access to tools like Siri and Google Assistant, which use natural language processing (NLP) AI to receive our voice commands, interpret them, retrieve and answer from the data, and respond to us according to what we have requested. Then, there are deeper levels of AI, such as Google's Deep Mind, which uses deep learning. "It is capable of making connections and reaching meanings without relying on predefined behavioral algorithms, instead learning from experience and using raw data as its inputs."[48]

Additionally, there are categories of AI applications, which are referred to as "Weak AI" and "Strong AI."

- **Weak AI** – This form of AI is designated as "weak" because developers have not yet developed it to the point of releasing its true potential. Also known as "narrow AI," it is non-sentient artificial intelligence, or intelligence applications that are developed to focus solely on one task.[49]

- **Strong AI** – This form of AI is designated as "strong" because it represents the maximization or true potential of AI, a state that we have not yet reached in AI development. Strong AI applications are able to, independent of human input, readily process and arrive at their own decisions. With the ability to process, behave and function more like human beings, these applications are able to apply their intelligence to solving multiple problems.[50]

The great strides that have been made in every level of AI have removed the limits from what we know is possible through technology, including how it can augment brain functioning. For example, I recently read an article in Science Alert entitled, "MIT Researchers Have Created a Bizarre Headset that Lets You Communicate without Speaking."[51] What I read about this new technology, which has been named "AlterEgo," blew my mind! The headset wraps around the ear and jaw of the wearer and is completely voice-free and hands-free. How does it work? It uses a process called "subvocalisation," which is what we call the activity of saying words in your mind but not aloud. Once these words are formed and register in your facial and throat muscles, AlterEgo picks up your silent speech using electrode sensors that are positioned on your face and around your jaw, processes this neuromuscular data, and then outputs a response. According to the developers, "Combined, the sensors allow the wearer to silently 'speak' to the computer by thinking words, and the computer to speak back via the headphones – like a Google or Siri you can talk to without having to say 'Ok Google' or 'Hey Siri' in a crowded street."[52] The technology is phenomenal; it even does arithmetic and plays chess!

Of course, when I see applications of AI like this, applications that serve as extensions of the brain, I can't help but consider the many ways in which the technology can be translated into helping the population that I am most passionate about – special education students. Understanding the vast, unlimited potentials of AI and how it can expand learning from being limited to a student's own cognitive functioning by providing access to a tool that serves as an extension of the brain excites me to no end! Through a marriage between AI and knowledge management in special education classrooms, we can literally change the life trajectories of students with CD!

A Look at How AI is Currently Being Used in Various Industries

Engaging AI is not only something that big companies and industries are doing "out there." Your own engagement with AI is closer than you think. For example, if you have an iPhone and use Siri or an Android phone and use Google Assistant, you are directly engaging AI: natural language processing. You ask Siri or Google Assistant a question, and they commence a search to find the answer you need as quickly as possible, delivering the results in only two or three seconds. These are considered "narrow" AI applications, because they are very tailored to specific outcomes like searches and getting you to your location. However, if you ask them to do so, they'll even ask you a riddle, tell you a joke, or pay you a compliment! Thus, if you've grown accustomed to talking to your phone and have grown reliant on it to give you accurate information, instructions and directions, you yourself have become dependent on artificial intelligence!

On a larger scale, AI has already infiltrated every major industry in some way.

Medicine

In medicine, AI is being used to help doctors evaluate patients' symptoms and diagnose diseases more accurately. Using AI to accomplish these tasks offers a more precise approach than using human intelligence alone. IBM, which is one of the industry pioneers that has developed AI software specifically for use in the medical industry explains:

> Before the widespread use of AI in medicine, predictive models in healthcare could only consider limited variables in well-cleansed health data. With AI, neural networks can process masses of raw data and learn how to organize that data using the most important variables in predicting health outcomes.[53]

As humans, it is impossible for doctors to review all of the latest medical research findings, clinical trial outcomes, and experimental treatments that are showing signs of success, as new advancements in the medical field are happening every day all over the world. How are doctors supposed to keep up with what's new and still maintain their responsibilities of serving their patients? The answer is AI technology. It can access and synthesize billions of pieces of medical information in a matter of a few seconds and pull it all together to assist doctors with providing a diagnosis and treatment plan that is more accurate and reliable than the doctor functioning based on his or her own intelligence alone. According to IBM:

Today, AI technologies such as IBM Watson are being used at Memorial Sloan Kettering Cancer Center to support diagnosis and create management plans for oncology patients. Watson is accomplishing these plans by effectively synthesizing millions of medical reports, patient records, clinical trials and medical journals. Watson's results are routinely 'out-diagnosing' medical residents in certain situations. IBM has also partnered with CVS Health for chronic disease treatment using AI technology. Johnson & Johnson and IBM are using AI to analyze scientific papers to find new connections for drug development.[54]

Additionally, IBM considers the use of AI in medicine to be important because:[55]

- It keeps researchers abreast of mountains of data (which is anticipated to double every 73 days).

- It provides contextual relevance for physicians, allowing them to easily access only the most relevant data needed at the moment.

- It improves clinical reliability, aggregating and producing results that physicians might easily overlook.

- It helps physicians to communicate objectively by presenting data and insights for them to consider.

- It reduces errors related to human fatigue because AI does not suffer from distractions, fatigue, or moods, allowing it to out-perform human accuracy.

- It decreases mortality rates by using its abilities to give greater priority to patients with more urgent needs and to recommend individually-tailored treatments to patients.

- It diminishes medical costs, as it is projected to reduce patient treatment costs by 50% and to significantly reduce human resource costs due to its ability to process millions of data and lab reports.

- It identifies diseases more readily with its higher level of ability to accurately analyze images like CT scans, x-rays, MRIs and ultrasounds faster than humans, allowing patients to start treatment faster.

- It increases doctor/patient engagement by reducing the amount of time physicians spend on desk work and data entry.

Unquestionably, the potential for the use of AI in the medical industry is clearly unlimited. AI's ability to interpret billions of pieces of text and image data using the most current medical research, extract data (even unstructured data) from peer-reviewed research publications to continually expand its medical intelligence, and consider variant information in the process of organizing all of this data so that it can be easily accessed by medical researchers and practitioners is priceless.[56]

Business

The use of AI is widespread throughout the business world, as industry leaders are always searching out ways to work smarter rather than harder, and to work faster in order to keep up with global market trends that literally change overnight. Integrating AI into their operations allows them to efficiently access solutions that improve their operations, reduce their costs, and increase their profits, which is always the bottom line for business.

AI in business is most commonly used in the areas of data analytics, automation, business applications, and natural language processing (which interprets the things we say as voice commands and responds to them accordingly). According to Harvard University report, "Automation alleviates repetitive or even dangerous tasks. Data analytics provides businesses with insights never before possible. Natural language processing allows for intelligent search engines, helpful chatbots, and better accessibility for people who are visually impaired."[57]

Nearly every segment of the business industry already uses AI at some level for such purposes as fraud detection, product recommendations, automated customer service and chatbots, forecasting human behavior, personalized marketing, and cross-referencing data.[58] Despite this wide range of AI use, according to Harvard Business Review, "AI stands to make the greatest impact in marketing services, supply chain management, and manufacturing."[59] Still, these sectors represent only a fraction of the business world in which AI can be fully maximized benefitting from AI's limitless analytical, comprehension and prediction abilities. Here are some specific examples:

Banking – AI is widely used in banking for fraud detection. If your bank account has ever been frozen because of suspected unauthorized activity or you've ever received a "Did you make this purchase?" notice pop up on your phone or email, you've engaged with this application of AI. Bankers give the AI software large quantities of sample containing both non-fraudulent and fraudulent purchase data to train the software on how to detect whether a purchase that shows up on a customer's account might be suspect or not. When it detects this likelihood, an ability that it becomes more adept at based upon what it learns about the customer's purchase habits over time, it notifies the consumer of the likelihood that fraudulent activity has occurred.[60]

Cybersecurity – AI is a key tool used by the security industry to detect anomalies. If you have any type of virus protection or security program installed on your computer, and you received a notice that the system has detected a problem, you've engaged with this application of AI. Cybersecurity has become a global crisis, and the techniques that are used to hack into computer systems and illegally access data have become increasingly sophisticated. The vast scope of the problem requires the use of AI to address it, as human programmers are no longer capable of handling the demand. Thus, AI programmers in this industry feed large amounts of data to machine learning algorithms (a method of analyzing data that builds models based on the technology's ability to learn from the data it is given, identify routine and non-routine patterns, and make a decision using little to no human intervention) and teach them to monitor activities, detect anomalies, react to perceived threats, and alert the users about the potential danger.[61]

Retail & Sales – AI is commonly used to provide customer service support in the retail sales industry. If you have ever gone online to make a purchase or to receive customer service from a company, and you used their chat feature online or their customer service number to reach them by phone, you've engaged with this application of AI. By phone, before you spoke to an actual person, you probably had to first interact with an automated AI application that asked you some questions and waited for you to answer so it could route your call to the right department. Online, when you clicked on the "Chat" button, a message probably popped up asking you how it could help you. After you indicated what you needed, it recommended a few automated solutions, and if these solutions didn't address your need, it allowed you to click "Chat with a representative" in order to reach a live person for further support. These AI applications were simply using natural language processing in both its written and audible forms to process the support you needed.[62]

Are You Ready to Make the Shift to Introduce AI into the Instructional Cycle?

In light of how AI has deeply permeated nearly every industry possible, the questions on the table for our consideration are:

1. Are you willing to subscribe to a different concept of what it means to "know" and "learn," shifting from a classical definition (the ability to access and process information intrinsically using one's own mind) towards a more innovative definition (the ability to access information from external resources) using AI?

2. Are you willing to witness the vast potentials of how AI can supplement the shortcomings of cognitively-disabled students in order to help them to "know" and "learn" better?

3. Are you willing to reclassify what it means for students with CD to be "educated" upon graduation, even if "educated" means that they can only find the information to answer questions and solve problems properly with the assistance of AI technology?

4. Are you tired of the dismal educational and post-educational outcomes that classical special education pedagogy has produced to the point that you are willing to explore the potential of AI to improve the education industry?

If we can answer "Yes" to each of these questions, we are also saying "Yes" to making the shift to integrate AI into the instructional cycle for students with CD. The same strides and advancements that AI has contributed to all of the other industries, helping them operate more efficiently, more effectively, and to produce better outcomes for them, AI can make for education.

TIFFANY'S STORY

Tiffany is in high school, and she has a moderate disability. Throughout her educational career, she has had difficulty learning math. Even though she is currently in the 12th grade, she only performs math at a 5th-grade level. Tiffany has a beautiful personality and likes engaging with people. This year, in talking with her parents and teachers, Tiffany indicated she wants to get a summer job. Tiffany's math teacher, Mrs. Simpson, recommended augmenting Tiffany's math skills with the use of a cell phone and a calculator. Mrs. Simpson taught Tiffany how to efficiently and effectively use these technologies in such a way that she could come up with the answer to any math question presented to her. Through diligent work in her math class, Tiffany can now quickly and confidently handle any math problem that may arise while working at a cash register. Tiffany is excited about looking for a summer job.

This is the power of AI in education.

WHAT IF...?

The Unlimited Potential Outcomes of Using AI to Manage Knowledge for Students with Cognitive Disabilities

When discussed within the context of special education, particularly regarding how we can fill in so many of the gaps that exist in serving students with CD, AI is one of the most relevant conversations that we can have. Why? Because the primary reason that the bar for what it means to educate special education students "to the best of their abilities" has remained so low over the years is that we haven't had the ability to raise it! Artificial intelligence is centered on helping us to "know" things more effectively without the use of the human brain. In the context of students with CD, individuals who cannot rely solely on their human brains to know things, we now have a mechanism to help them know things another way – through AI technology. In a nutshell, by using AI to augment the learning of students with CD, we can essentially extend their knowing – or learning – capabilities beyond that of the individual person's brain.

The Proposed Shift in Knowledge Management: An Innovation Blending the Classical and Technological

You'll notice that I've used words like "shift" and "innovation" as I refer to the changes that I'd like to see in special education classrooms through the integration of AI. This is intentional language. My desire is not to turn the current special education system on its head and then kick it out the door, radically re-placing it with something that we've never seen before. Instead, I'm advocating for a shift. If you're like most people, when you think about a "shift," you don't think radical; you think of a sub-tle movement to the right or the left in a way that keeps the original form and function of things largely intact. The same is true for "innovation." This term tends to conjure up images of making alterations to a product or process that exists while largely preserving its original form and function.

This subtle shift is exactly what I am proposing for how we in-novate the management of knowledge in the special education classroom. The reality is that knowledge is already being man-aged for students with CD. I'm simply proposing an innovative shift in how that knowledge is managed to produce greater learning outcomes for students with CD. Another reality is that technology is already available in schools, but it is accompa-nied by a clause that basically says, "The student can use it but not become dependent on it." What I'm offering is a knowledge management shift that says it's totally okay to integrate a depen-dence and constant reliance upon technology into the learning process for students with CD.

The approach in which this shift is grounded is not a this-or-that solution. In fact, the framework functions best by acknowledging that there are two different types of learning opportunities – the classical learning approach that we currently use and the augmented learning approach in which AI is used as an extension of the brain – and then blending the two in order to produce the best possible learning outcomes. It's not about throwing out one so we can incorporate the other; it is innovating the former to make accommodations for the latter.

Can You Imagine?
What Life Could Look Like for AI-Empowered, Students with CD

The impetus of this book is to propose a shift in how we educate students with CD, and the main point of the shift is "how" we implement the use of AI in students with CD. Without the shift, AI will only benefit what's already being done across industries, and education will miss out on the opportunity to shape innovation. If we make the pedagogical shift to allow AI innovation to help shape education, it stands to revolutionize the learning and life outcomes of students with CD. I'd like for you to take a moment and try to visualize what the future would look like if we were courageous enough to embrace innovative, new approaches to ensuring that these students received all of the support they needed through AI technology in the classroom.

If we make the pedagogical shift to allow AI innovation to help shape education, it stands to revolutionize the learning and life outcomes of students with CD.

Imagine a future in which David, an 8th grader, has a severe cognitive disability, but his classmates do not view him as disabled. With the aid of technology, David does grade-level work like everyone else in the class. David has been using AlterEgo, a personal assistant for two years. He uses AlterEgo to silently query the internet for information and then uses that information to assist him in all of his classes, including math, history, and Spanish. By trial and error, David has learned where the limitations of the AlterEgo are, and he has concentrated his skill development in those areas. David is confident about his future, and most important to David, he does not view himself as entirely dependent on others for success!

Imagine a future in which Melanie has a moderate cognitive disability and is excited about entering 9th grade. Melanie has had her learning augmented since elementary school. Because this is her first year in high school, Melanie's parents, Emilie and Tayor, have scheduled a meeting with Melanie's teacher and counselor. Melanie's parents have been pleased with the increased skill level she has been able to achieve with technology through middle school. In high school, Melanie's parents want to assess Melanie's ability to perform in the kind of realistic situations she is likely to encounter after high school. With this in mind, her parents are requesting that Melanie not be given extra time or content modifications on her in-class assessments. Emilie and Tayor will use this information to shape Melanie's goals after she graduates from high school. They think college or a trade school will be a realistic option for her, but they want to make sure.

Imagine a future in which Dr. Zackery Johnson has just been hired as the new principal for Hightower Middle School. It is a magnet school for augmented learning. The school has 900 students, and 40 percent of these students are in special education or are using AI-augmented learning to support their education. Dr. Zackery is excited about this new job! As an AI magnet school, Hightower attracts the best human resources in the teaching professions, those who enjoy seeing the dramatic impact technology has on the lives of children with cognitive disabilities. Dr. Johnson smiles, remembering back to a few years ago when this school population would not have been his first job placement choice. Now, he can't wait to see all that the innovative AI approaches can do to transform the learning outcomes of the students he serves.

Here's the good news: these types of scenarios are not far off in the future. In fact, with technology, they are possible today because the future is here now!

What If...?
The Limitless Potentials of Integrating
AI Technology into the Instructional Cycle

Have you ever taken the time to envision what life in special education and integrated classrooms would look like if they were driven by a heavy emphasis on using AI technology for learning? Consider the following potential not-so-futuristic scenarios.

What if a student with CD could be given a computer, tablet, or phone to access Microsoft Word or other speech-to-text programs during a reading activity in class? The speech-to-text program reads the electronic, written content aloud to the student. Further, imagine that same student using a Finger Reader, which is a wearable tool that attaches to the finger to help read text. There is a small camera on the Finger Reader that will scan text and give real-time audio feedback of the words it detects. It would also notify the reader, via vibrations, when the device is at the start of a line, end of a line, moving to a new line or when the user is moving too far away from the text baseline. Imagine how much more advanced that student's comprehension of what is written in the books on the classroom shelves would be at the end of the semester compared to a student who did not use such technology.

What if a child with a moderate learning disability could be given permission to use their computer or phone, with the aid of software, to participate in classroom writing assignments and assessments? The word processing functions of the software (like Microsoft Word) could predict words, check passages of text contextually, read text aloud using TTS technology and recognize split and merged words. It would also include an integrated dictionary for the student to quickly lookup a word and specialized learning software like Ghotit Real Writer & Reader Software, designed specifically for students with disabilities. Imagine how much more advanced this student's ability to produce high-quality writing would be over those of other students who have the same disability but do not use such software.

What if, in math class, a student with CD is allowed to use their calculator to complete math problems for an assignment or assessment? Instead of memorizing math timetables, the student would be taught how to complete specific types of problems using a calculator. In addition to using a calculator, the student would be taught to use MathTalk, a speech recognition software program for math, that can help students with a range of disabilities. From pre-algebra to Ph.D. level mathematics, the student would be able to perform math problems by speaking into a microphone on his/her computer, because MathTalk works with Dragon NaturallySpeaking software for voice-to-text functionality. If the student was blind or had vision disabilities, they could use the integrated braille translator to understand what numbers, facts and figures were before them. When the teacher assigned math simulations (video or animated simulations that allow students to see how a math concept or problem would work visually) the student could work through the problem and then see the result play out in the simulation. If the classroom was not equipped with such advanced technology and only had access to a virtual assistant like Amazon's Alexa, the student could easily use this technology to learn and complete math problems. Imagine how higher this student's scores would be for assignments and assessments versus those of their CD counterparts who did not have access to such technology in the classroom. Also, imagine the confidence and enthusiasm that the student would have when stepping into math class, knowing that he/she was fully equipped to be able to find answers to the questions that the teacher asked.

AI's Integration into the Learning Cycle: What It Looks Like from Preschool through High School

The primary goal of making the shift towards augmenting the learning of students with significant cognitive disabilities with AI technology is the following: to teach the child to facilitate AI technology as a customized tool that they can use in their daily interactions in such a way that it helps them to break through the learning plateau that arises as they matriculate through secondary education. During this stage of their education, such augmentation becomes especially necessary because this is where larger and larger gaps begin to emerge in learning and performance between students with CD and their non-disabled peers. *When effectively instructed on how to use AI, this technology becomes an extension of their minds' abilities to remember, store facts, and draw upon those facts to perform a specific task.* How the integration of AI in the classroom looks from stage to stage of education varies and should be examined closely.

Using AI Technology in Preschool and Elementary School

Throughout preschool and elementary school, it is important that the child develop as much skill for learning as possible without the use of AI technology. During these years, highly-skilled special education teachers use instructional strategies to address any CD-associated learning problems that their students might have. The child's educational progress is dependent on such intervention, and this early assistance, establishes the foundation for all future learning. However, content mastery is not the sole overarching goal of education at these early grade levels. Instead, at these earlier ages, the goals in the classroom are for the child to be able to socialize with peers appropriately and to begin to learn to read, write, and do basic math and begin to learn about their disability. Most importantly, at this early age, they need to learn to perform these skills without the assistance of technology.

Technology can be used to a limited extent in the classroom with younger children with cognitive disabilities whose parents opt for them to participate in AI-augmented learning. For children in preschool and elementary school, this augmented AI instruction simply looks like teaching students the basics of using a computer, including how to log on and off, open a file, save a file, access the internet, and generally work a computer. However, teachers also teach the students without cognitive disabilities how to use the computers in the classroom in the same way. As a result, at these early grade levels, the instruction for students with CD on an AI-augmented track versus for students without any cognitive disabilities are quite similar.

With the shift that I am proposing toward the augmentation of learning using AI technology, I am not proposing that we inundate preschool and elementary school children who are diagnosed with a cognitive disability with technology. Instead, I would argue that, for preschool and elementary school students, technology use remains the way it is in its current state. Currently, the computer is used as an instructional tool by the teacher to enhance and reinforce learning for students who do and do not have cognitive disabilities. The approach, called "Computer Assisted Learning" or "Computer Assisted Instruction," is used to assist the student as he/she learns in real time. It is available, as needed, on a self-paced schedule and can also be used in group work, which fosters collaborative learning among students.

For example, in preschool and elementary school, teachers use instructional assessments to measure what the child is able to achieve without the use of technology. While the child may learn through teacher-led instruction and supplement this learning by using some sort of guided instruction on a computer, when they are tested on what they have learned, they are tested on their ability to recall and use instructional content in context without the aid of technology. That is, they can use technology to help them in their learning, but they cannot rely on technology to help them during their testing or assessments. Thus, although computer technology is used in the classroom, it is used for the purpose of helping the students function on their own. It is designed to be a supplement that helps them learn fundamentals on their own so that they do not begin relying on technology to accomplish these learning goals at such an early age.

You might be thinking, *Is it fair to test students with CD on what they have learned when they clearly have a challenge that hinders their learning?* This is a good question. The reality is that all children have the ability to learn, including children with cognitive disabilities. The difference is that children with a cognitive disability are hampered in their cognitive ability to perform and excel at or above the same rate as their non-disabled peers.

However, even though their performance is hampered, they can still perform. They can still take assessments, and they can still implement the skills that are being assessed. The assessment given to children with disabilities simply shows the content that the child has mastered through the filter of their disability.

Using AI in Middle School

It is not until middle school that the shifts that I am proposing for AI-augmented learning be implemented in the classroom for children with cognitive disabilities. Upon entering middle school, it is time to build upon the basic reading, writing and math skills that the student learned in elementary school solely using their own cognitive skills. Middle school, however, begins the building phase of education, and in this phase, AI can be used to augment the child's learning by serving as an extension of what they know and can do or accomplish on their own. In this context, AI switches from being simply an instructional tool that is used to help the child learn (as it was used in elementary school) to being a personal support tool that they can use to improve their educational outcomes.

Now that they are in middle school, children with cognitive disabilities can begin to use technology as an ever-present support that serves as an extension of the child's mind. This technology can vary, including anything from a computer, to a phone, to a tablet or other personal computing device. Students with CD are able to use these technologies to obtain and use information in proper context, like responding to a question or implementing an action. Additionally, when taking tests or assessments, they use these same technologies (without the assistance of anyone else) to access the answers to questions. What has been discovered is that when students with CD are trained on how to access answers using technology and are permitted to use the technology on assessments and exams, their response rate for answering test questions is nearly the same as their peers who do not have disabilities. The reason for this is clear: the computing device allows students with CD to bridge the gap in performance that would otherwise exist between them and their non-disabled peers.

Using AI in High School

In high school, a student with CD will be taught how to lean on AI technology in the classroom to not only access information but to use the information in context to solve problems that might occur in real-life situations. At this stage of education, students will begin focusing their studies on becoming proficient in using expert AI systems in one or more specific fields of study, augmenting their efforts to reach these proficiencies through technology. For example, they might choose to focus on math, science, history, or language arts, mastering how to use AI technology to get to the more complex answers they need about these subject areas quickly and accurately. Mastery of at least one expert system in a specific field is required for high school graduation. Additionally, in order to graduate with their high school diploma, these students must demonstrate that they can meet the same academic proficiencies as their non-disabled peers. They will, however, be permitted to use technology (unassisted by anyone else) to complete these assessments of their proficiencies.

Managing Our Expectations: What AI Will and Will Not Do for Students with Cognitive Disabilities

As we begin to seriously consider a shift towards AI-augmented learning in the classroom, it is important for us to manage our expectations of what it will and will not accomplish in the lives of children with cognitive disabilities. This will not only help us to look for feasible outcomes rather than impossible ones as we evaluate the impact of AI-augmented learning, but it will save the program from being dismantled prematurely because it doesn't seem to be working.

1 | It Will Not Create Geniuses

First, AI-augmented learning will not create geniuses out of students with CD. It would be outstanding if AI could accomplish this with our children, but it simply cannot. What it can do, however, is help students who have cognitive disabilities realize more of their potential to excel in both their educational and post-educational contexts relative to their non-disabled peers. While learning to function with a dependence on AI technology might not completely level the playing field for individuals with CD and those without CD, it will at least position those with CD to compete in the job market and make lifetime earnings commensurate with their counterparts who do not have CD.

2 | It Will Empower Students to Access Information Efficiently

Second, AI will empower students with CD who cannot come up with answers to questions using their own brains to access the answers through technology, but this will not erase the need for learning in the classroom. It is what is learned by students with CD that is the focus in the AI shift. For example, if you've ever used Amazon's Alexa or Apple's Siri, you know that you can't just start talking to these devices and expect them to answer. You had to be taught how to address them properly so that they could know how to fetch whatever information you needed or perform whatever function you requested. In the same way, giving students with CD complete access to information does not mean that they will be able to mindlessly sail through their classes without having to learn anything. Instead, the instructional emphasis will be placed on teaching them the parameters that they need to master in order to search for and retrieve the information they need in order to answer the questions on an assignment or exam.

To be able to access information efficiently (not spending 30 minutes to retrieve an answer) and effectively (coming up with the right answer) and to meet high standards of performance in the classroom (keep pace with and compete alongside the rest of the class), a baseline level of knowledge is needed. For example, have you ever searched for information on the internet and could not locate it, even though you knew it existed somewhere out there? Better yet, have you ever found some information that was offered in response to your search query and realized that you weren't able to use it? Perhaps you couldn't find the exact piece of information that you were searching for to address your specific need, or perhaps what you found did not offer sufficient detail to meet your need. Or, maybe all of the information that was returned in your search results was just too much, so much so that it overwhelmed you and as much as you tried, you couldn't sift through the avalanche of information that was thrown at you. When all was said and done, how long did you search for that one piece of information before you either gave up? How many times did you go back and change the keywords and phrases in the search bar in order to give the search engine new parameters of what information to seek out for you?

These examples should help you to understand that even though access to information is readily available, locating the information you need to answer a question or to apply to a certain context is a lot more challenging than one might initially think. In the same way, accessing information through technology is not a walk in the park for students with CD; being able to access the information they need efficiently and effectively still requires significant skills on their part. They will have to work just as hard for their grades in the class. It's just that the kind of work that they do – the work of accessing information – will be different.

3 | It Will Not Replace the Need for Teachers

Another expectation that we must be careful to avoid is that of being able to rely so heavily on the technology to produce successful outcomes for the students that we no longer have to rely on teachers to play a role in the educational success of students with CD. The use of AI as augmentation for children is not going to remove the need for the critical role that skilled teachers play in the instructional process. Actually, the opposite is true: teachers will be more critical to successful outcomes. In their book, *Human and Machine: Reimagining Work in the Age of AI*,[63] Paul Daugherty and James Wilson outline activities that will be exclusively the domain of humans. This domain includes activities such as leading, empathizing, creating and judging, among others. Humans will always be necessary in the age of AI, and they will work in cooperation with AI machines through training, explaining and sustaining activities rather than competing against them. In exchanges, machines will amplify human skills and allow greater interaction between humans and machines.

Translating the work of Daugherty and Wilson into the educational arena, teachers will be needed to provide leadership and to empathize with children about their learning progress, growth, development, and mental health throughout the educational process. Teachers will also assess children's overall progress toward educational development. Ultimately, AI will amplify the knowledge base that children with cognitive disabilities can access for information and help them apply that information in its proper context through the use of AI expert systems. These AI expert systems, which are designed to emulate the decision-making of a human expert in a subject-specific field, are designed to provide reasoning skills based in various bodies of knowledge. I'm sure we can all agree that this is pretty advanced! However, despite how advanced or sophisticated these AI expert systems become, they will never become as advanced as an actual human teacher who can provide the intangible touches that a child with cognitive disabilities needs in order to succeed in the classroom.

4 | It Will Change the Connotation of "Disability"

Finally, another expectation that we must manage as we embark upon making the shift towards AI is that of how leaning heavily on AI will impact the ways in which individuals with CD are viewed. We cannot expect people who are prone to mock individuals with disabilities to start equating "student with a cognitive disability" with "brainiac" simply because the student begins using AI. Instead, a more reasonable expectation is that AI-augmented learning will change the connotation of "having a cognitive disability" from meaning "dumb" to meaning "capable with augmentation." That's exactly what the power of AI does for individuals with CD: it makes them capable of doing so much more when they are aided by technology than they could have ever hoped to accomplish, in school or in life, on their own.

That's exactly what the power of AI
does for individuals with CD: it makes
them capable of doing so much more...

99

MARK'S STORY

Mark has dysgraphia, which causes him to have difficulty writing. Mark's favorite subject is social studies, because he loves reading about faraway places. However, lately, Mark has been struggling to do well in social studies. Mark's teacher, Mr. Zolenski, uses an integrated teaching strategy. Mr. Zolenski requires students to read, complete a short writing assignment based on the reading assignment, and then engage in a brief discussion. After consulting with the special education teacher about Mark's challenges, rather than have Mark skip the writing portion of classroom assignments, Mr. Zolenski now requires that Mark complete writing assignments on his tablet or the classroom computer. Mark's tablet has Microsoft Word, and the classroom computer has the writing program Ghotit Real Writer & Reader, specifically designed to help people with dyslexia and dysgraphia. The Ghotit program learns from Mark's past mistakes, personalizing suggestions for spelling and grammatical errors. Ghotit also predicts words, checks passages of text contextually, and recognizes split and merged words. It includes an integrated dictionary for Mark to quickly lookup a word as well. Since using Ghotit and Word, Mark is excited about social studies again, because the writing assistance technology helps him keep pace with the learning of his peers!

This is the power of AI in education.

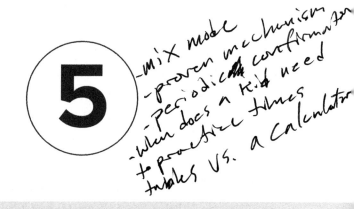

-mix mode
-proven mechanism
-periodica confirmation
-when does a kid need
to practice times
tables vs. a calculator

AN UNFAIR COMPETITIVE ADVANTAGE?

The Equity Debate in the AI/CD Conversation

To equitably integrate the use of AI as a link working in tandem with a student's disability, it will be necessary to create a framework of when, how, under what circumstances, and to what extent AI should be used to augment a student's education. I call this the "AI Augmentation Index." The function of this index would help us to understand how much a student with CD should access technology based on need. The measures on the index would range from low intelligence/ low use of technology to high intelligence/high use of technology.

Of course, overall, I advocate for low intelligence/high use of technology among students with CD, but an index is necessary, because neither CD nor special education is monolithic; there are students with varying degrees of intelligence in different special education settings, so our approaches to helping them to engage AI technology to augment their cognitive functioning and learning experiences must be as individualized as they are. Having the AI Augmentation Index at our disposal will help with this.

For example, if we are working with a third grade student with cognitive disabilities, we must ask ourselves questions like:

- How much access to brain-augmenting technology does this student need between now and graduation to help him/her attain learning outcomes high enough to be able to apply for and function in college?

- In which classes, contexts, and under which circumstances should the student's access to using AI technology as an extension of his/her brain be limited, if at all?

- What does AI technology access look like for this student, including the software, equipment, and usage behavior based on his/her individual capacity?

Still, the dominant question that people are compelled to ask is, "Is *any* use of technology to augment a student's learning, even in a special education classroom, fair to the other students in the school or the district?" People who ask this question are wading into the waters of intense equity discussions that have been occurring all over our nation for decades. Let's take a moment to understand the major themes in the equity debates.

learning or
assessment?

> "Is any use of technology to augment a student's learning, even in a special education classroom, fair to the other students in the school or the district?"

Fairness, Equity, and Equality:
The Central Issue of the AI-Augmented
Learning Debate

Let me start by explaining that fairness, equality, and equity are often confused. Especially in discussions about education, people assume that equity is the same as equality and that equality equals fairness. However, each of these has a different meaning. According to the Merriam-Webster Dictionary:

- **Equality** is the quality or state of being equal, as in of the same measure, quantity, amount, nature, or status; regarding or affecting all objects in the same way.[64]

- **Equity** is justice according to natural law or right, dealing fairly and equally with all concerned.[65]

- **Fairness** is lack of favoritism toward one side or another, or the quality or state of being marked by impartiality and honesty; freedom from self-interest and prejudice.[66]

Both equality and equity positions are leveraged by people to support their beliefs about what is fair, or what counts as fairness. Fairness is a fundamental value that is hard-wired into every human being. According to psychology researcher Melanie Killen, "Extensive research has shown that fairness is a core value for individuals across a wide range of cultures, including those that are traditional and modern, urban and rural, and of high and low socioeconomic status."[67]

From the time of our infancy and throughout our childhood, we begin developing concepts about fairness and justice. While you might think that these moral judgments are shaped in us solely as a result of our interactions with our families, our environment, and our cultural norms, research shows evidence of the contrary. Instead, a number of study findings indicate that very early in life, children begin constructing these judgments that value the necessity of what is fair and devalue harm to others, considering it wrong, before these values are directly taught or transmitted to them by their families and the external environment.[68] Then, as we continue to progress through life, deliberate attempts are made to further reinforce our values of fairness, socializing us to believe in its "rightness" and its necessity for the civil, peaceful and effective functioning of families, groups, and society.

I'm taking time to explain the value of fairness because it is critical to understanding the lenses through which people interpret equality versus equity. Our inclination toward fairness is something that has been driving us since infancy, before our earliest recollections. As a result, it's a hot button issue, something about which people tend to become incredibly passionate. When they perceive that an individual or group is being treated unfairly, something in them rises up, and they feel deeply compelled to defend what they have been conditioned to believe is morally right. The problem is, two people can look at the same situation, and based on their orientations, one can perceive that one approach is fair while the other believes that the other approach is fair. Herein lies the dilemma that divides the two schools of thought regarding whether it is fair to allow students with CD to augment their learning in special education classrooms.

People generally tend to believe that all people should be treated equally, a characteristic known as "a natural human aversion to inequality."[69] They base their belief that everyone should be treated exactly the same way – equally – because this is the only way to truly keep things fair. However, in some cases, equal treatment is unfair. For example, let's say you're about to feed two dinner guests. The first dinner guest hasn't missed a meal in years; he's had breakfast, lunch, and dinner every day for as long as he can remember. The second dinner guest has a different story. He has been homeless for a year and has only managed to scratch up a morsel to eat a few times a week, so he is starving. Would it be fair to treat them equally at dinner, giving them exactly the same amount of food, or would you say that it's only fair that the starving man receive a little more? If you say that the starving man should receive a little more food at dinner because of his condition, you are making an argument for equity.

- All arbitrary when tools are unlimited

Here's another example. Let's say there is a high school comprised of 9th – 12th grade, and to graduate and receive a regular diploma, you have to master the content in each grade. We want everyone in high school not to drop out and successfully complete each grade so that they can go on to attend college, or a trade or professional school. Now, let's say we have three students, but each of these students is performing at varying grade levels: one student with CD who is performing three grade levels below his peers; one regular education student performing on grade level; and one advanced studies student performing three grades above his peers. If the goal is to have everyone graduate with a diploma and with equal potential to pursue additional education so they can maximize their earning potential over their lifetime, are we going to provide the same instructional supports to each student (the equality position), or are we going to modify the instructional supports provided to each student (the equity position)? This, is, however, a trick question!

At first glance, you may say that schools across the nation already fall into the equity position because instructional supports are different for each of these three groups of students: the student with CD has special education, the regular student has a regular curriculum, and the advanced studies student has an above-grade curriculum. However, if schools are currently operating from an equitable stance, why, then, are the current outcomes for each of these three groups not equitable? Consider for a second that, maybe, current educational practices are not as equitable as we believe. If each of these students is standing on instructional supports of varying heights for their needs, imagine that the box the student with CD is standing on for support is made of straw, and the student is falling through the box!

My point here is that on the surface, education might seem to believe in equity and might even appear to be operating from an equitable position toward meeting the needs of students with CD, when in reality, neither is true. Subscribing to the erroneous perception that education already operates with equity toward students with CD is not harmless; it is dangerous. Why? Because people who operate with this understanding believe that the equity issue has already been addressed for students with CD and have thus become numb to the issue of advocating for equity for this special population. As a result, these students receive neither the attention, nor the advocacy or resources they need to help them achieve better educational outcomes and an equal chance at succeeding in life.

While equality ensures that everyone receives the same treatment and allotment of resources regardless of differences or deficiencies, equity ensures that everyone receives what they need by taking these differences or deficiencies into account when allocating the distribution of resources. There are also conditions surrounding whether people perceive allocating resources based on equality to be fair versus allocating resources based on equity to be fair.

Research indicates that people tend to believe that allocating resources equally is fair "when there is no obvious basis for differentially distributing resources. Under these conditions, everybody is considered equally deserving and unequal distribution is considered unfair."[70] On the other hand, people tend to believe that allocating resources unequally, or based on equity, to be fair when this unequal distribution of resources is based on the recipient's need, or when their differences merit a difference in resource allocation. According to one study:

> People are generally happy to have more resources allocated to individuals with special needs. Or, if a pre-existing situation has resulted in unfair inequality, people generally prefer to allocate future resources unequally to correct or minimize this inequality. Under these conditions, some individuals are considered more deserving than others and unequal distribution is considered fair.[71]

Now, let's transition this discussion of equality versus equity into the educational setting. If we say that all students in all of the classrooms in a school should be treated exactly the same way, including the allocation of resources, concessions, and considerations they receive to help them achieve high educational outcomes, we are arguing for equality. However, we cannot overlook the fact that not all students and all classrooms in the school are the same. There are some classrooms in the school, namely the special education classrooms, containing students who have greater need because of their cognitive deficiencies. The differences that exist between them and students without cognitive deficiencies positions them to need a greater allocation of resources, concessions and considerations in order to achieve high educational outcomes. Thus, we are making an argument for equity, or the unequal allocation of what is necessary to give students with cognitive deficiencies what they need in special education classrooms to achieve high educational outcomes. Their differential treatment, which is based on their deficiencies, is only fair.

Educators largely tend to consider equity to be a fair approach in schools based on two primary conditions: unequal learning needs between students and unequal student backgrounds. The first, unequal learning needs, acknowledges that students who are in the same grade level, around the same age, and have had the same access to learning opportunities for about the same number of years might still vary in their learning ability and educational development. Therefore, we cannot hold them to the same path toward meeting performance standards and expectations, and we cannot teach them the same things in the same ways. Teachers generally recognize this in the classroom, catering their approaches to each student's need rather than treating all students equally. That is, they give students with a more advanced ability to learn a lesser allocation of their classroom resources (time, individualized attention, etc.), because they require less to help them achieve high educational outcomes. Then, they give students with a less advanced ability to learn a greater allocation of their classroom resources, because they require more to help them achieve high educational outcomes. In the end, because of the equitable approach, all of the students in the classroom receive what they need to achieve high educational outcomes. The consistency of high educational outcomes could not have been achieved in the classroom if the teacher was committed to equality, that is, giving all students the same amount of time and individualized attention, regardless of their learning ability and educational development. According to equity in education researchers, Masters and Ray:

From this perspective, students are treated 'equitably' when their unequal starting points are acknowledged and when attempts are made to differentially meet individual needs. Rather than expecting all students to reach the same point in their learning at the same time, every student is expected to make excellent progress in their learning, regardless of their starting point.[72]

The second condition in which educators largely tend to consider equity to be a fair approach in schools is when there are unequal student backgrounds. Under this condition, educators acknowledge that all students have not had the same access to education, the same quality of education, or the same learning opportunities. These disparities might exist due to class differences, geographical differences, socioeconomic differences, or other differences; it is a known and well-documented fact that these factors affect students' access to and quality of education. For example, if a student lives in an upper-class community, there is a strong likelihood that the combination of local tax dollars that the student's parents pay, when combined with state funding, results in a well-funded educational system that provides access to a higher-quality education for the student. Conversely, that student's counterparts that live in lower-class communities do not have an ample supply of local tax dollars, and when combined with state funding, often results in access to a lower-quality education for its students. Lower-quality education for students in lower-class communities occurs in many states, despite state school funding formulas designed to compensate for districts that have fewer local tax dollars.

You've probably seen the debates about resource allocation based on unequal student backgrounds on your local television news, because it's an issue all over the nation. The fundamental question is this: should school funding be allocated equally across all school districts, or should school districts that already have more financial resources receive less school funding and districts that have fewer financial resources receive more school funding? Which is fairer? Financial resources necessarily determine the quality of education that students receive. In light of that, should students who were born into disadvantage automatically be destined for a lower-quality education and the lower-quality job options and lifestyles that subsequently follow, while their peers who were born into class privilege are destined to receive a higher-quality education and the higher-quality job options and lifestyles that follow? Even though low-SES students have no control over the socio-economic contexts into which they are born, should they be doomed to pay a penalty for it with a poor-quality education?

Masters and Ray's perspective is this:

> In an 'equitable' school system, students' special needs and unequal socioeconomic backgrounds are recognized and resources (for example, teaching expertise) are distributed unequally in an attempt to redress disadvantage due to personal and social circumstances. Here again, 'equity' is achieved by prioritizing fairness over equality.[73]

Hopefully, if you did not understand fairness and equity before, you have a much better understanding now. Just in case you're wondering why I've gone to such lengths to help you grasp these concepts, the answer is simple: the argument in favor of using AI in CD classrooms to augment student learning is all about equity-based fairness.

I mentioned before the need for developing an AI Augmentation Index, a framework that will help us determine when, how, under what circumstances, and to what extent AI should be used to augment a student's education. Now that you understand equity, you understand that these measures will vary based on each individual student's need. Still, there is the question about whether allowing any students in a school to use AI to augment their learning, regardless of where they fall on an AI Augmentation Index. To be fair, I'd like to examine both sides of the debate.

AI Augmentation of CD in Special Education: The "For" Argument

Proponents for using AI in special education classrooms to augment the learning of students with CD couch their argument in the idea that it's all about equity. Yes, it is true that only certain students in the school will be able to rely heavily on technology to help them access answers to questions in the learning environment, but they should be given this concession – the consideration – in light of their cognitive deficiencies. Yes, it is also true that if students who do not have cognitive disabilities were able to rely heavily on technology to help them access answers in the same way, they could excel above and beyond their current performance. However, to counter an initiative that proposes the use of an educational supplement that will help to compensate for the deficiencies of students with special needs with "Well, if you're letting special needs students use AI technology, you need to let our students without CD use it too, because it's only fair that if one group gets to use it, everyone gets to use it!" is an equality argument.

Based on what we have learned about equity, particularly how there are some students who start their educational journey at a significant advantage, we are obligated to give students with CD a greater allowance of dependence on AI technology than other students in the school. The goal is to get all students to meet academic milestone proficiencies by the time they graduate.

-use my mm m type model to allocate type and time of lesson

Students without CD can do this without assistance; students with CD cannot. The fact that students with CD were born at a disadvantage, having challenges that exist along a continuum from mild to severe, places them in a position to require additional assistance in order to achieve the same goals as their peers who do not have CD.

The pro argument for using AI technology in special education classrooms to augment the learning of students with CD is that these students deserve to use whatever they need in order to access information their brains cannot produce. Without having access to AI augmentation, students with CD will lack the knowledge they need to function independently in the future, and if they cannot function on their own, at some point, we as a society will pay the price for it with our tax dollars.

I happen to know that there are some parents who resist the idea of implementing the use of AI in classrooms to augment the learning of students with CD because they feel that their own children will be put at a disadvantage if the school gives this technological advantage to special education students. However, students without CD should not feel threatened by their peers with CD using AI technology, because their peers with CD will always remain at a social and educational disadvantage, even with AI augmentation. You see, augmenting the learning of students who have CD with AI technology is not a cure-all. It's not going to turn students who can barely add single-digit numbers into math prodigies. All it does is helps them to access the information that they need to answer questions so they can achieve greater academic outcomes in the classroom and greater survival outcomes in life!

I like to use the example of building a rocket. As intelligent as I consider myself to be, if someone dropped me in the middle of a big aircraft hanger with a bunch of parts and step-by-step instructions on how to build a rocket, I probably wouldn't be able to do it. I might get some of it done, but even with the answers written on the instructions in plain black and white right there before me, the likelihood of me being able to follow them to build a rocket is quite low... and if I did manage to build something that even remotely resembled a rocket, I can guarantee that you wouldn't want to risk your life by flying in it! My point in this example is that we must be careful not to overestimate what giving people access to information can produce. Just because you provide someone with a lot of information doesn't mean that they will be able to understand it, use it for the purpose for which it was intended, or leverage it to accomplish something worthwhile. Access to all the information in the world will not automatically translate into comprehension, awareness, analysis, usefulness or any other intellectual outcome that we value.

Here's another example. Have you ever been in a class in which the teacher announced that you were going to take a test, but you were allowed to use the book to answer the questions on the test, and this made you so comfortable that you didn't study at all because in your mind, you were just going to crack open the book, find the answers and make a score of 100%? If you've ever done this, you probably failed the test or came close to it just like so many before you who operated on a fatal, flawed assumption: just because the answers were available to you, you thought you'd be able to easily access the right one with enough speed and efficiency to ace the test. It was only after you walked out of the classroom defeated by an open-test, of all things, that you realized that just because someone tells you that you can retrieve the answers you need from some place other than your own memory doesn't mean that academics will become super easy or that you'll be operating at genius-level intelligence! It's much more complex than that.

When students with CD use AI technology to augment their learning in the classroom, it is true that the technology will provide them with a wealth of information and will also help them to access answers from a source other than their own brain. However, even with their heavy reliance on technology to access information, they will still be at a significant disadvantage relative to their peers without CD. Their peers without CD are able to do so much more with the information they access from their own brains than students without CD, things like analyzing, synthesizing, problem solving, creating, inventing, and so much more. No matter how much AI technology we give to students with CD to access the answers, even if we allow them to become heavily dependent on technology in the classroom, students without CD who do not rely on technology for the answers will always be giant leaps and bounds ahead of them. Maybe someday, technology will close the gap between what the human mind can do and what AI is capable of, but we are not there yet.

Finally, those who advocate for the use of AI in special education classrooms base their position on their concept of empathy: anyone with any sense of empathy would want to see individuals who are already at such an extreme disadvantage equipped with tools that will at least make them able to function as independent adults. They feel that people who do not support students with CD augmenting their learning with AI are essentially saying that they don't care that there exists an opportunity for students with CD to attain better learning outcomes. Instead, students with CD should not be allowed to use AI because students without CD are not allowed to use it, because it's just not fair.

AI Augmentation of CD in Special Education: The "Against" Argument

Detractors against using AI in special education classrooms to augment the learning of students with CD couch their argument in the idea that it's all about equality: every student should have equal access to the same tools and resources, regardless of differences, because this is the only fair approach. According to this position, if students without CD can't use AI to augment their learning, students with CD should not be able to use it either.

The fact that you're able to comprehend what you're reading at this moment is an indication that you do not have a cognitive disability. You have the intrinsic psychological capacity for rationality and autonomy, and these requisites are the foundation for your claims for education, fairness and a good quality of life – a life worthy of respect and dignity. You have worked hard to learn and have used the knowledge you have gained to produce good outcomes and make valuable contributions to society. However, you need to be careful to not fall into the trap of apathy, mercilessness, and disdain that the privileges and opportunities of the "self-made" life you enjoy can lay for you. I call it the "Us vs. Them" trap.

As a person without a disability, people can tend to view individuals with cognitive disabilities – those who do not have the rationality and autonomy of "regular people" – as individuals who have not earned the right to access the best that society has produced. The belief is that "they" do not deserve such access (to things like technologies that can improve their lives, for example) because "they" have not contributed to its creation like people like you have. The individuals without disabilities see themselves as "regular," and the disabled as "irregular" – the "others." Therefore, individuals without disabilities can feel that it's not fair to give individuals with disabilities "shortcuts," allowing them access to the best society has to offer. The best society has to offer was produced by the "regular" people, and they do not feel that they should have to share these benefits with "irregular others" who had no hand in producing these advancements. When you fall into the "Us vs. Them" trap, you are also prone to live by the "Ours vs. Theirs" argument. If you succumb to these ideologies, you will stand opposed to individuals with cognitive impairments having access to AI-augmented "shortcuts" in the classroom because it gives them an unfair advantage when competing with their peers without disabilities in the classroom. You'll also stand opposed to the cognitively impaired being able to compete with individuals without disabilities in the workforce, because the individuals with CD can augment their functioning with AI and their non-disabled peers cannot. Without openly declaring it, you'll actually be fully subscribed to the idea that the individuals with cognitive disabilities are not even fully human. After all, if they were fully human, then they would not have missing cognitive functioning, which is the essence of being human.

To those who have fallen into the "Us vs. Them" trap and operate by the "Ours vs. Theirs" mentality, allow me to bring a few things to clarity for you. Just because individuals have a cognitive disability does not mean that they are not deserving of being considered a whole person that is deserving of dignity and respect.[74] Who elected you, an individual without a disability, the judge and jury of what it means to be fully human and deserving of the best society has to offer? According to researcher and advocate Eva Feder Kittay, individuals with disabilities, including those who are severely and profoundly disabled are, first and foremost, human beings. Despite their mental challenges, they are no less human or worthy than you. Individuals with disabilities do not have to "earn the right" to equal access to resources or to the best of what society has created. Not having a disability does not give any individual without a disability the right to appropriate goods, power and other privileges based on their discretionary judgment of who is deserving or not.[75]

People on the "Against" side of the AI-augmented learning debate tend to be those who have not had to live with deficiencies or disadvantages that have hindered their abilities to progress in life, so they are blind to the difficulties of doing so. Further, as a result of being able to move through life so easily with little to no resistance, they consider themselves to have gotten ahead and achieved success in life simply by virtue of their own hard work and determination. There is no acknowledgement of the privilege they have enjoyed and how this privilege has helped to facilitate their success, because they operate out of a position of advantage rather than a position of deficiency.

Over the years, I've found that the most empathetic people tend to be the ones who have had their lives impacted by being disadvantaged by virtue of how they were born at some point, and the least empathetic, most indifferent and merciless people tend to be the ones who have never had to deal with any disadvantage at all. This latter group tends to fall into the camp arguing against the use of technology to boost the learning outcomes of students with CD. They hold their ground based on the position that the cognitive deficiencies that these students have are a personal problem that should be addressed by a personal solution and that the students without CD and their parents shouldn't have to "suffer" for the bad hand that students with CD have been dealt in life. The detractor's declaration: "It's not my fault that those special education kids have the deficiencies they do. What's fair is fair. My kids can't use technology to find the answers, so no one else's kid should be able to use it either!" They hold to the position that life is not fair, but the school environment (at the very least) should be as fair and equal in its treatment of students as possible.

The next point in the argument against allowing the learning of students with CD to be augmented with AI is that school is a competition. According to this position, the belief is that every single student in the school is competing for the same top class rankings, academic awards and accolades, scholarships, and college admission slots, and allowing any of the students in the school to lean on technology in the classroom gives them an unfair competitive advantage in what should be an equal competition. They speculate that if students with CD are permitted to use AI to augment their learning, they will make higher test scores and better grades than their non-CD counterparts, ultimately attaining a higher class ranking and lowering the class rank of students without CD. In sum, people in the "against" camp tend to perceive that allowing students with CD to use AI in the classroom will make them an academic threat to the student body – a threat that would not exist absent of the use of AI – so such augmentations should not be allowed. I shouldn't have to tell you how faulty this reasoning is when it comes to special education students.

We cannot forget the dynamic of the human condition in student academic achievement. Students without CD have a wide variance in their ability to perform; some students assert themselves and choose to be scholars, while others just barely pass to the next grade. They have the same classroom opportunities, but some take more advantage of them than others. Students with CD are no different; AI does not change this dynamic of the human condition. Some students with CD will use AI to become outstanding students, while others will use AI to just barely make it. However, even the students with CD who assert themselves to the best of their abilities will, by no measurement, become overnight scholars. AI simply allows students with CD to begin to realize more of their academic potential when measured against the same academic standards as their peers who do not have CD with the same academic rigor.

The reality is that some students with CD will compete with students without CD in the school for top graduation spots and college acceptance letters. However, there will also be others with CD who are competing against themselves to be able to do the most basic things like ride the bus on their own without getting lost and learning how to give a proper greeting and farewell to people as they enter and exit a store! Again, when we overestimate the advantages that students with CD will gain if they are permitted to augment their learning with technology, we run the risk of immersing ourselves in unrealistic fears. Every student with AI-augmented learning will not be super smart any more than every student without CD will have a 4.0 GPA. Students with CD are people first.

Ultimately, your ability to define "fairness" in this debate rests on the way you answer a few essential questions.

- Is it fair that before he/she even enters first grade, a child with a cognitive disability is destined to have lower overall life outcomes?

- Is it fair that there is a fix available to help individuals with cognitive disabilities experience far superior educational and post-education outcomes compared to current outcomes and yet withhold this fix from them for any reason at all?

- If you were a student in school and had a cognitive disability, would you want access to AI technology to help improve your learning outcomes, especially knowing that your entire post-education future was riding on how well you were able to master certain concepts in school?

At the heart of the matter, I am advocating that the non-disabled – the decisionmakers and distributors of resources based on their own notions of fairness – consider a potential approach to achieving equity in the learning and lifelong outcomes of individuals with CD. This is something that is attainable, because we now have the resources to make such outcomes feasible! With one bold, courageous decision to stand on the side of equity-based fairness using AI-augmented learning, we can *literally* change the current and future quality of life for individuals with cognitive disabilities. It's our choice, but it's their lives. When I speak of equity here, I am not proposing the elimination of any rights that have been gained for individuals with disabilities (the Individuals with Disabilities Education Act, Section 504 of the Rehabilitation Act, or the Americans with Disabilities Act). Instead, I am proposing an additional path forward that offers additional avenues for potential growth for the cognitively disabled, allowing them to compete in education and future employment with their non-disabled peers. This can be accomplished using the collective intelligence of the human race that has produced breakthroughs in science and technology that are fueling the emergence of AI as a method to augment the brain of individuals with disabilities so they may actively function, compete and excel on par with a person without a disability.

By law, schools are required to give special education students everything they need for learning, and it is clear that this population needs more resources to achieve learning than their counterparts who do not have CD. By nature of having a cognitive impairment, the educational starting point for children with a cognitive impairment is different from the starting point for children without a cognitive impairment. Equitable education means providing the type of learning support during the educational process that ensures that everyone has approximately the same potential for learning and future outcomes.

Equity is not simply accepting that some individuals have severe cognitive disabilities that result in poor learning outcomes and others are geniuses that can produce great learning outcomes. What is equitable is that everyone is given access to the tools and resources that they need in order to be their best by producing the best outcomes they are capable of producing. Prior to AI emerging as a tool to support cognition, there was no way other than strategic instructional practices to improve the learning outcomes for students with CD. However, now that we have AI, we have technological tools and resources that can level the playing field and help students with CD compete, achieving the same educational and post-educational outcomes as their non-disabled peers. Equity is the foundation of fairness; it recognizes differences and manages these differences for the maximum benefit of everyone. Life is not fair, but societies can choose to make life equitable.

JAMAL'S STORY

Jamal is a twelfth-grade high school student who reads at a sixth-grade level. In school, Jamal has been using a Finger Reader to augment his reading ability. The Finger Reader is a device worn on his finger that reads words aloud when Jamal points to them with his finger, allowing him to listen to the words through earphones. This device has proved invaluable in helping Jamal make the most of his reading skills. Jamal has been able to access twelfth-grade reading material and engage with his peers, and this has provided a tremendous opportunity for him to learn new content. With confidence, Jamal hunts for a summer job like his peers without fear that his reading skills will limit what he can accomplish. Jamal applies for a job in his local library reshelving books, a job that he would have struggled to do well without the assistance of the Finger Reader. As an added benefit, while shelving books, Jamal has found several new topics of books he usually would not pick up. Jamal is now in the habit of reading and checking out books from the library!

**This is the power of
AI in education.**

DETAILS

Critical Considerations for the Implementation of AI-augmented Learning in Special Education Classrooms

Remember the beginning of this book when I admitted that although I had lots of questions, I didn't have all of the answers? That's still true. This book is meant to lay out a lot of questions for your consideration so that they may spark critical conversations that are necessary to bring greater definition to the AI-augmented learning shift that I am proposing.

The most important consideration regarding implementation of AI in special education classrooms is this: we must begin where we are. Start simply. AI consultants suggest that when a company or organization is considering how to leverage AI, the first step is to take an inventory of which parts of the organization's operations are able to be digitized. Dr. Mark Esposito, co-founder of Nexus Frontier Technology and the instructor of a Harvard University program entitled, *Artificial Intelligence in Business: Creating Value with Machine Learning*, recommends, "Rather than dreaming up a magic-bullet solution, businesses should consider existing technology that can free up resources or provide new insights." Noting that AI implementation starts at the company level, not with AI, he recommends that the very first step, or the "low-hanging fruit" for companies is recognizing how they can improve on how to do the things they already do in their day-to-day operations.[76] Then, after AI is integrated into different aspects of the business, it can scale up its use, building and expanding upon the uses of it in the organization.

In an article on the use of AI in business, Harvard University provided a prime example of taking such an approach:

> Amazon is... an early adopter [of AI]. Even before its virtual assistant Alexa was in every other home in America, Amazon was an innovator in using machine learning to optimize inventory management and delivery. With a fully robust, AI-empowered system in place, Amazon was able to make a successful foray into the food industry via its acquisition of Whole Foods, which now uses Amazon delivery services.[77]

As you can see, Amazon started simply (at least, what is considered "simply" for Amazon!) and then scaled up its use of AI. What does this mean for us? How do the "start simply before scaling up" and target the "low-hanging fruit in implementation" concepts translate into our efforts to integrate the use of AI into the instructional cycle of special education classrooms? How can we ensure that we are both realistic and strategic in our implementation?

Starting Simply: A Foundational Framework for the Most Basic Level of AI-Augmented Learning Implementation

At the most basic level of implementation, I have a foundational framework for what a special education program that uses AI to augment the learning of students with CD looks like. It consists of the following phases.

Phase 1:
Diagnosis & Selection of AI-Augmented Learning Option

The child is identified as a child with a disability under the Individuals with Disabilities Education Act (IDEA). Consequently, the child is now officially entitled to receive all of the protections afforded to a child with a disability. As an enhancement to the child's learning program, the parents or guardian of the child may choose to elect to have the child's learning augmented by AI. This option can be made during elementary or middle school.

Phase 2:
Placement in Special Education Classroom that Provides Training on Use of AI Technology

The child would be placed in a classroom with teachers trained on AI-augmented learning along with other students with disabilities. Teachers would receive training on how to teach students to use AI to access information or answers, a process which could vary for different subject areas. In this classroom, the child would be trained by the teacher on how to effectively use whatever AI technology tools and resources the school has available to access answers and information they need in the classroom (by subject). Depending on the severity of the CD, the child may only spend an hour or two a day in this setting, or the child may be immersed in this setting for the full class day to promote effective skill development.

Phase 3:
Integration into Mainstream Classroom with Permission to Augment Learning Using AI Technology

After the child demonstrates a baseline mastery of being able to use AI to access information and apply it to answer questions in proper context, they are removed from the special education classroom and integrated into a non-CD, mainstream classroom. The goal is always to get these students back into an integrated classroom setting, because they need to grow accustomed to real-world settings. In the real world, they're not going to have a community of their own; they will live among and have to learn how to interact with people without CD. When they leave the educational setting, they will be working, learning and engaging with people who do not need AI to augment their functioning. Thus, they might as well get used to navigating this more realistic, integrated context, complete with all of its academic and social challenges. Mixed environments are considered positive because they help to teach students with CD social skills, how to get along with other kids without disabilities. The benefit of teaching them these skills in the classroom is that an instructor or counselor can coach them through any issues they might face, preparing them for the real world. Placing students with CD using AI-augmented technology is also beneficial because it's not a one-sided benefit; it's a mutual one. When given the opportunity to interact closely with students with CD, students without disabilities learn that these students are able to perform just like them and their peers without disabilities; the only difference is, they need a little help.

Phase 4:
Application & Evaluation of Student's Capacity to Increase Learning Outcomes Using AI

Teachers in the integrated, mainstream classroom will encourage the child to use the AI tools in order to access information and apply it to answer questions in the proper context. The child will be encouraged to use AI augmentations for class assignments, assessments and homework.

Phase 5:
Ongoing Training & Support to Fine-Tune and Expand Student Use of AI

As the child's skills in a subject area increase, additional AI training (outside of the non-CD, mainstream classroom) will be periodically necessary to sharpen the student's information search and information recovery skills.

Controversial Questions Surrounding the Basic Implementation of AI-Augmented Learning

Should parents be allowed to opt in or opt out of their students with CD participating in the AI track?

I previously mentioned the need to develop an "AI Augmentation Index" that would help to determine how much a student with CD should access technology based on need. The measures on the index would range from low intelligence/low use of technology to high intelligence/high use of technology.

	LOW	HIGH
LOW	Low Intelligence Low Technology	High Intelligence Low Technology
HIGH	Low Intelligence High Technology	High Intelligence High Technology

Figure 1. AI Augmentation Index

After students with CD take an assessment, the results would indicate whether they should use technology and how much technology they should be able to access for classroom learning, assignment completion and test taking. However, what if, after a student is tested and rated according to the AI Augmentation Index as needing high use of technology, the parents decide that they do not want their child to participate in the AI-augmented learning? Should parents of students who require high use of technology on the AI Augmentation Index even be given a choice of opting in or out of using augmentation? If the child is in a special education classroom in which the teacher leads the class in a manner requiring technology and all the other students use AI technology for learning, what would happen to students with CD who opted out?

At what grade level should we begin augmenting learning using AI?

Children are generally diagnosed with having a mild to moderate cognitive disability between around the 3rd, 4th and 5th grade, when they begin missing developmental milestones. In more severe cases of CD, a diagnosis can be made much earlier. At any point after a child receives a formal diagnosis of having a cognitive disability, schools can make AI-augmented learning available to these students. However, should they?

There is no clear answer or recommendation to when we should begin augmenting the learning of students with CDs using AI. There is only question after question. For example, is there an age or grade level that's too soon to begin teaching students to rely heavily on AI technology to learn? Do we stick to the status quo that really doesn't begin integrating AI into the learning cycle in a significant way until middle school? Is there such a thing as starting children too early, so early that technology use hinders their brain development and cripples their capacity to learn on their own? Should we at least allow students to matriculate through elementary school and wait to begin augmenting learning with AI in middle school? Then, there are other questions. If we introduce AI augmentation as a necessity for basic functioning in the early years of a child's life, whether elementary or middle school, will their heavy reliance upon technology hamper the development of their social skills? If so, should we wait to begin AI technology augmentation in high school? Better yet, should we only allow low degrees of AI augmentation in elementary school, a greater degree of AI augmentation in middle school, and an advanced degree of AI augmentation in high school? There are so many questions to answer surrounding when AI-augmented learning should begin. Each of them is sure to be a hot-button debate with passionate supporters and detractors defending their sides based on their views of what is right. Again, I don't have all of the answers. My job is to raise questions for consideration and discussion, and the issue about when to begin teaching a dependence on AI is sure to be a controversial one when the time comes.

Can students with CD who participate in the AI track be allowed to hop on and off the track for certain grade levels or classes?

People once subscribed to the myth that wearing eyeglasses makes the eyes dependent on the corrective lenses, and over time, glasses weaken the eyes. According to the Mayo Clinic as well as myriad other researchers, this is only a myth. If you have to wear corrective lenses for your vision to function better, even after years of use, your eyes neither grow weaker (as a result of the glasses, at least), nor do they solve the original vision problem you had in the first place.[78] In the same way, some will argue that if we allow students to be on the AI track for several years and then take them off of the AI track for the last years of school, their cognitive learning skills will have been weakened through a heavy reliance on AI technology. Although this belief is unsubstantiated – and mythical – they use it as grounds to say that once students are placed on the AI track, they are forever destined to remain on the AI track. They say that it will be impossible for students to one day get off the AI-augmented learning track and function without technology because this learning style will cripple them from operating any other way. However, is this really true?

The reality is that this is a policy discussion that needs to occur. Policymakers need to hash out whether students will be allowed to alternate between being on the AI track and not being on the AI track. If students can hop on and off the track, are there certain times when they can make this transition? Will they have to wait until the end of a semester or a school year, or can they hop on or off in the middle of a semester? Will certain grade levels offer hop-on and hop-off privileges while others do not?

Then, policymakers will also need to determine whether selecting to use AI-augmented learning can be course-specific or whether all of a student's learning has to use augmentation during an entire semester or school year. For example, can a student choose the AI-augmented option just for math class, and continue learning in the traditional, classical way in all of his/her other courses? If not, why not? If so, how would we address the perceived unfairness of the students without CD who are struggling to come up with the answer using their own brains sitting next to the students with CD who whip out their phones or tablets and gain access to the right answer in record time? Again, these are important conversations that need to take place now as we prepare for implementation.

Should the AI track be available to all students to choose, whether or not they have CD?

Brace yourself, because I'm about to say something here that I know will be controversial to most. When I propose augmenting the learning of students with CD using AI technology, this is only the starting point. I don't think that we should limit the benefits of this technology just to students with disabilities. After we refine the use of AI technology among students in the CD population, I believe that other students – students without CD – should also be able to use AI technology to augment as a mode of learning, too. Allow me to explain before you proceed with planning to crucify me.

There is the idea that scientists will, at some point, create a computer with a level of AI that exceeds the intelligence of the human brain. The fear – although an unlikely one – associated with the idea is that if a computer can outthink the human brain, the computer could potentially arrive at conclusions that humans would not agree with and order actions that could result in danger, destruction or demise of an individual or group in some way. If we do not understand how the computer's AI is processing data and arriving at these conclusions, we cannot control it. We would be subject to it, and our safety and well-being as human beings will be at its mercy.

If the first thing you think of when you hear the term "AI" is "killer robot" you've probably watched too many sci-fi movies! You know, the ones in which scientists built computers that became so smart that these computers began to outthink and outwit their developers in dangerous ways, refusing to be re-programmed, controlled or shut down, wreaking havoc and threatening to destroy the world.

While it is within the realm of possibility that such situations could occur, AI experts have called for more research on how to prevent these potential scenarios from becoming a reality. Allow me to assuage your fears by explaining a few reasons that computers with above-human level AI will not take over the world. First, developers are intentionally working to prevent such a future by integrating active controls into AI processors' contingencies, which disallow such things from happening. Second, researchers are developing a second path into these technologies that augment the human brain, offering a counterbalance with above-human level intelligence into computers. Also, humans using AI augmentation will also have above-human level intelligence completely under their control, thus narrowing the gap between human level intelligence and strong AI.

In 2015, an open letter on artificial intelligence, which was signed by notable experts such as Stephen Hawking, Elon Musk and dozens of other technology leaders, advocated for expanded research to occur in order to avoid the potential dangers of AI. However, one notable thing that is absent from the letter is a *ban* on AI.[79] AI is recognized as having immense benefits for humanity, but along with those benefits comes the responsibility to mitigate risk. The AI community and experts are actively working to balance the risk of AI with its benefits to humanity.

We must do the same, moving forward in our development and use of AI technology without allowing the fears of its potential paralyze us with fear.

The fundamental principle behind my belief that all students (not just those with cognitive disabilities) should be able to use AI technology to augment their learning lies somewhere inside of these potentials. Augmentation, in general, allows humans to extend their capabilities, learning and knowledge so they can perform at a higher level than they normally would. When we teach students to use AI, immersing themselves in understanding it at its deepest levels through personal use, we produce individuals with limitless potential to develop the most brilliant AI technology possible that is controllable, by design.

In light of this, I envision an educational landscape with instruction occurring on two learning tracks. The first track, which is the classical, non-AI-augmented track will be about reviewing, analyzing, synthesizing and creating information and knowledge. There will always be benefits to the classical track of education, so it should never be dismantled. The second track is the non-traditional AI-augmented track. This track approaches learning with a different set of objectives like learning to take large data sets and extend knowledge by drawing conclusions based on patterns, or applying knowledge and facts to a dizzying array of factors and circumstances and using these approaches to produce positive solutions to society's most pressing challenges.

When it's all said and done, the main question that we must answer is, "What does this mean for the individual student?" In other words, what will the student be able to accomplish with and without using an augmented track? What does the student see him/herself doing after high school (going straight to work, starting a business, college)? What does the student want to specialize in career-wise, and which track will prepare him/her best for it (augmented or non-augmented)? Regardless of a student's level of need for AI augmentation, the student's decision to choose the classical or augmented learning track will not be the determining factor in his/her success. Ultimately, when these students graduate from high school, they will need some form of additional development, whether in general or industry-specific job skills training or college.

There are strengths and benefits to both learning tracks. While the classical track is about teaching students facts and the ability to analyze information in an efficient and accurate manner to be innovative, the augmented track is about the ability to quickly access, manage and manipulate huge swaths of data and information in complex and intriguing ways that produces novel data-based solutions. That said, should we offer both tracks in school simultaneously, allowing parents and students to choose their preferred track? It's a hard question, but this should not disqualify it from consideration. If we could only shift our thinking away from the fears of allowing all students access to AI-technology augmented learning and instead focus on the unlimited potentials and returns it would provide for our society, we would all stand to benefit greatly.

Policy & Pricing: Essentials to Consider When Planning to Make the Shift

There are many changes and considerations that need to be extensively discussed, decided upon, and fleshed out at district, state and national levels before the full-scale implementation of AI can occur. I classify these considerations into two categories: policy considerations and cost considerations. The questions we must answer about the ways in which we will shift how technology is used in education fall under policy considerations. The discussions that we must have regarding how schools will get their hands on these technologies and ensure that they are universally available to all the students who need them fall under cost considerations.

Policy Considerations in Making the Shift Towards AI-Augmented Learning

Testing & Evaluation Considerations

Then, there are questions about tests, like, "How do we test students with CD who use AI technology to get answers?" and "What does that assessment look like?" My thought on this is that we are going to be testing the speed at which students can access the required, relevant information in context as well as the speed and context in which they are able to use the answer. Thus, the benchmark for testing would be, "How long does it take the student to access the answer and use it in context?" Keep in mind our previous example of how easy it is for people to fail open-book tests, because having open-access to the information needed to answer questions does not automatically translate into one's ability to quickly locate the relevant information needed to answer the test questions.

The gold standard for me is setting up a system in which students become so proficient in accessing relevant information in an efficient manner that they meet or exceed the progress of their non-CD counterparts on exams. I don't dream of this so that they can increase their class rank or enhance their eligibility for a college scholarship but so that they will have a greater chance of sustaining themselves later in life. Never lose sight of the big picture here. Our goal with using AI to augment the education of students with CD is so that they will become skillful in information retrieval in the classroom, increasing their capability of accessing the information they need to take care of themselves in life. Without a proficiency in accessing the relevant information they need to navigate real-life situations, they could end up like so many other millions of people with cognitive deficiencies who live below the poverty line, or even worse, homeless, after their primary caretakers are gone.

Graduation Considerations

There are likely to be parents who feel that students who use AI technology to complete their assignments, take their tests, and make their grades should be automatically disqualified from competing against the other students in the school who did not have the benefit of using AI technology in their learning process. They will feel that these students' grades shouldn't be considered in the class averages, in setting curves, for the limited number of slots in the school's National Honor Society, or even in academic rankings that qualify students for graduation honors and distinctions. Whether their concerns are valid or not is a matter of debate. It is one of many policy discussions that must be held as we continue to work through what this whole thing looks like and how it will operate.

Another point that we will have to discuss and come to agreement about is whether the high school diploma of a student without CD will look exactly like the diploma of a student with CD. That is, when students with CD who used AI to complete their assignments, take their tests, and ultimately graduate, should there be an asterisk on their diplomas indicating that, unlike their peers without CD, they completed school using AI to augment their learning? Some might say that this will make students with CD stand out and differentiate them in hiring decisions from their peers without CD. I have news for you: they already stand out from others. This is a policy issue that is up for discussion.

I personally don't think that it would be a bad thing for students who graduate using AI technology to augment their learning to have an asterisk on their diploma. But then, why use such a small symbol that this student graduated using a different process? What about making their diplomas a completely different color, a universal sign that it belongs to a student with CD who is fully capable of independent functioning using AI technology. It's just an idea, but I think it might be a good one. Not everyone sees having CD as a negative thing. Not all people subscribe to the stigma. There are some employers who might actually *want* to know when a job applicant has CD and has graduated based on AI-augmented learning, because hiring these individuals would contribute to a sense of diversity, inclusion and empathy in the workplace. Again, as long as the person can do the job well, even if doing the job well requires dependence on technology, that's all that matters.

Finally, as we consider the policies that will shape how the shift is implemented, we must consider what systems need to be in place to ensure the seamless transition of AI-dependent students with CD into colleges and universities. These students have matriculated through elementary, grade and high school with a heavy dependence on technology to achieve their learning outcomes. In light of this, will the colleges' systems have to necessarily allow for the use of AI in the classroom for the students with CD to continue to succeed? Whether or not these accommodations would be required by the state for state-funded colleges and universities would be a matter of policy – another critical policy consideration. My position is that these concessions would definitely need to be made for students with CD in order for them to be successful in their higher education courses.

In an earlier chapter, I discussed what it means to learn and know things. Colleges and universities are like other educational institutions; they're locked into teaching students to learn and know solely through using their own brains, and they consider learning and knowing things any other way to be cheating. This is where training comes in: we need to educate the educators. The development of systems that help students with CD transition seamlessly from high school to college must necessarily include re-orienting educators' perceptions about "learning," "knowing," and "cheating." Doing so will ensure that college professors do not stigmatize, penalize, or operate with a negative bias toward students with CD for their dependence on technology during classes or when taking tests.

Additionally, policy discussions should include what type of system or program must be developed to make a smooth transition for students with CD graduating out of the care of the public school system and into the care of the college system. There should be no gaps in the process, because gaps are dangerous things that students with CD could fall through. If gaps are present in the process, some students with CD might never make it to college after a successful AI-augmented high school career.

For example, it would be essential to have a formal, programmatic handshake system in place on the college campus that:

- introduces students with CD to the support staff responsible for their well-being on campus

- familiarizes students with the college campus layout

- helps students identify and register for courses that are endorsed as AI-technology friendly

- identifies a support network on campus that may include professors or other students who are sophomores or older to help students with CD brush up on their skills with integrating AI into their learning environments

- assists students with accessing various hardware and software technologies that can augment their learning

- ensures that any other supports that are needed are in place to make for a seamless transition necessary for students with CD to be successful college students.

Ideally, the goal of an AI-augmented secondary education is that a student with CD can function in any college course with any professor. Again, this is just another discussion among a wide range of others that must take place around the table during policy considerations.

Employment Considerations

One of the first things that we must consider in the discussion about employment considerations is which types of community programs need to be in place to educate local employers about students with CD and how they learn. These programs must ensure that employers know that students with CD who have graduated from the local high school using AI-augmented learning will need to continue using this technology in order to perform effectively at work if they are hired. An essential part of this training is managing employers' perceptions about the use of AI so that they do not see it as cheating, as an unfair advantage, as preferential treatment, or as an employee spending time on his/her phone instead of working. Other employees might use their phones to chat, scroll, and waste time, but employees with CD need to be able to use their phones as an exception to the "no phones while on the clock" rule in order to access information, answer questions and get answers. The same goes for other types of technology tools available now and in the future. Employers must be taught to embrace technology as a necessary supplement to these students' functioning. If this message is effectively communicated through employer education programs, they will accept that using AI technology is an extension of their potential hires' brains, necessary for them to meet or exceed the job performance of their counterparts in the workplace. This should also lead to greater levels of patience, accommodation and consideration after hiring individuals with CD.

It all starts with education. Educating employers about how to work with students who rely on technology for their functioning should have some clear, measurable outcomes, beginning with employers hiring more students with CD. These students can be hired to work part-time jobs during the school year and full-time jobs during the summer. Whereas their CD once rendered them unable to get a job or function in the workplace, receiving training on how to use AI technology to augment their functioning will not only equip them to be successful in the classroom but in the workplace.

In general, when people receive a high school diploma or a college degree in our society, this certificate says that they now possess basic proficiencies and that they can perform at a certain level. The same type of diploma or certificate will be in place for students who have gone through the education process using AI technology. At a base level, when they graduate from high school, their diploma is going to vouch for their ability to meet certain competencies, whatever they may be. This is something else about which local employers need to be educated. When a job candidate with CD comes to apply for a job with a diploma in hand, employers will automatically know that the individual might not be able to do everything all of the other non-CD employees do, but he/she can at the very least perform a certain list of functions with the help of AI technology. The key is to educate employers about what the diploma of a student with CD means before they are presented with these documents in the hiring decision. With the proper proactive education, employers will learn how to properly assess job candidates with CD who are leaving education and going into the workplace as well as how to properly accommodate them as they strive to fulfill the job function for which they are hired. As long as they can get the job done well and efficiently – even if they are using AI to do it – that's the only thing that matters!

Pricing & Funding Considerations in Making the Shift towards AI-Augmented Learning

There are questions concerning cost that must necessarily be discussed before we can ensure the widespread, equitable integration of AI technology into special education classrooms. These are discussions that should occur simultaneously with policy-level and instructional considerations. For example, what will the cost of the full-scale implementation of AI in CD classrooms look like in terms of financial and human resources? While I do not have the answer to questions like this, I do not anticipate any part of this to be a "quick and easy" process; it could take three to four years for policies about cost and curriculum to be ready for full-scale implementation. What we do know for now is that technology is the wave of the future in education, and it will need a formal funding source, not just for students with CD, but for all students.

Technology is the wave of the future in education, and it will need a formal funding source, not just for students with CD but for all students.

Right now, in education, schools are required to provide anything that is needed for the effective education of a special education student to learn. This requirement is powered by the Individuals with Education Act (IDEA), which requires a free and appropriate education that is tailored to individual needs for any student determined to be a student with a disability. It is also powered by the Every Student Succeeds Act (ESSA), which was signed into law in December 2015. The legislation gave each state the flexibility over determining how it educates its students, including students with disabilities. Specifically:

> ESSA requires that all students, including students with disabilities, have access to a well-rounded education and be held to high academic standards that will prepare them to succeed in college and careers. ESSA grants states significant flexibility over the design of their accountability systems, but encourages the use of more college and career readiness measure of student success.[80]

If our advocacy is effective and policymakers arrive at a consensus that AI technology is needed to augment special education student learning, these resources could come at a high cost. After all, we're talking about technology, and technology is not cheap; there will inevitably be some tools and resources that will require a financial outlay. The quandary becomes about how to fund AI technology needs for students with CD when revenue at the local, state and federal level is often fixed and insufficient to cover such expenses. For example, in the 2016-2017 school year, overall, there was $330 billion from local revenue, $346 billion from state revenue and $60 billion from federal sources, accounting for a total revenue of $736 billion.[81] Of the $60 billion from federal sources for elementary and secondary education, $13.6 billion was targeted for special education services provided through the Individuals with Education Act. Although this might seem like a lot, it is insufficient. This $13.6 billion, which represents the current funding for IDEA, still falls short of the full funding level that Congress intended with the law when it was enacted. Full funding of IDEA would be 40% of each state's cost for special education.

Potential Avenues for Increased Funding to Cover the Costs of the Shift

While there is no magic solution for the shortage of additional special education funding necessary to implement the integration of AI into classroom learning for students with disabilities, there are potential avenues for additional funding at every level.

Federal Level Proposal 1: Fully-fund IDEA

At the federal level, while IDEA funding from year to year has been relatively constant, Congress has not fully funded IDEA. When Congress first began funding special education in 1975, it was designed to cover 40% of the cost required to educate and provide services for each child. Currently, the federal portion of IDEA funding (currently $60 billion) is below 15% of the cost required to educate and provide services for each child. Getting IDEA fully funded requires Congress to act in accordance with IDEA's published guidelines, increasing the federal funding to the 40% designated in the Act. You can show your support for the full funding of IDEA by writing your congressional representatives and voting for political candidates, at every level of government, that support special education.

Federal Level Proposal 2: New IDEA Funding Allocations Earmarked for Technology

Congress is required to reauthorize IDEA every five years. IDEA was last reauthorized in 2004 and was amended in the

Every Student Succeeds Act in December 2015. IDEA was supposed to be reauthorized in 2019, but Congress agreed to delay its reauthorization that year. Although there is no official date that reauthorization will occur, it will likely be taken up by Congress within the next one to two years. Whatever the timeframe, when Congress begins its next round of discussions about IDEA reauthorization, another avenue toward increasing special education funding is to introduce formal consideration of "new funding allocations" specifically earmarked for the purchase of technology for special education classrooms. Again, you can show your support for these new funding allocations by reaching out to your congressional representatives and asking that these funds, which could be used to acquire AI-driven tools and resources for both teachers and students, be allocated equitably across states so that all students can have access to the technology they need to augment their learning and increase their educational outcomes.

State & Local Level Proposal 1: Factor Technology into the Funding Formula

At the state and local levels, many school districts and states currently use funding formulas to determine how funds are distributed to schools. I propose adding in additional technology factors into those formulas. For example, funding formulas typically include items like:

- Administration supervision

- Teaching

  ◊ Regular school

  ◊ Students with disabilities

  ◊ Occupational education

- ◊ Special school
- ◊ Pre-kindergarten

- Instructional Media

  - ◊ School library and audiovisual
  - ◊ Educational television
  - ◊ Computer-assisted instruction

- Pupil Services

- Attendance

- Health Services

- Interscholastic Athletics

- Pupil Personnel Services

School funding formulas attempt to account for state and district revenue and differences among districts with the goals of ensuring adequate and equitable funding across schools. As AI becomes more prevalent in education, particularly the education of students with CD, it will become more important to differentiate how money is allocated for technology. Beyond the catch-all category of "computers," it may be helpful to differentiate between computers, tablets, learning software, AI technology and network infrastructure that supports all of the resources that make internet connectivity, communication, operations and management of technology in an educational setting possible.

State & Local Level Proposal 2:
Offer Tax Credits to Corporations Partnered with
CD Classrooms for AI Development & Research

In addition, state legislatures may consider offering corporate tax credits for high-tech companies that are working within elementary and secondary school settings to conduct research and development on AI technology, or that are working on infrastructures that support AI use and development. If state legislatures consider providing tax credits for companies engaged in such activities, it will be important that the tax credit program is structured so that companies receive the tax credits only *after* having met the criteria to qualify for the credit. It will also be important for states to have an existing structure in place to monitor and enforce provisions of tax credit stipulations and laws.

> Providing equitable funding for students with CD to gain access to the technology they need to augment their learning has to be a non-negotiable.

State & Local Level Proposal 3:
Ensure the Equitable Distribution of Funds & Subsidies

Providing equitable funding for students with CD to gain access to the technology they need to augment their learning has to be a non-negotiable. Remember my example about physically disabled people needing wheelchairs? Without wheelchairs, they cannot get around. Wheelchairs are not benefits, privileges or luxuries; they are necessities that are required for these individuals to be able to function. We should view access to AI technology tools the same way; students with CD need them to function. Thus, ensuring that all students have access to the AI tools that they need is not providing them with a luxury or a privilege but with resources that are necessary for basic functioning. Ensuring that these resources are distributed equitably to schools is key; if funds are, instead, allocated equally, some students will have access to the AI technology they need while others will not. Because of the necessity of having technology to function, it is not an option that any student with CD to not have access to these tools in school.

Then, there's also the issue of providing access to AI technology for students at home. Physically disabled people who rely on wheelchairs to function do not only need access to their wheelchairs at school; they need them at home, too. In the same way, students with CD will not only need access to AI technology at school; they will need this access at home. I think that a part of the cost considerations that are discussed regarding the normalized integration of AI technology into the life of a student with CD is how to ensure that the access they have to this technology in school extends into having the same access at home. Some families of students with CD will be able to afford the technology without any assistance, but students from families without the financial resources to afford it should not be penalized because of their socioeconomic status. Again, access to technology for students with CD is not a luxury or a privilege; it is a necessity required for adequate basic functioning. Thus, every student with CD, regardless of class status, should be provided access to this technology, both at school and at home.

Also, consider that I am not proposing that we subsidize these individuals for life, only while they are in elementary and secondary school. If we provide them with access to the AI technology they need during secondary education and teach them to use it effectively, after they graduate, they will have a potential for greater success as they seek additional education at a two-year, four-year, or professional school or enter the job market. Equipping students with CD with AI technology helps to prepare them for the job market and for earning competitive wages that will allow them the ability to thrive, prosper and pay for their own AI technologies, which they will continue to need for basic functioning in the future.

State & Local Level Proposal 4: Encourage CSR Donations from Corporations & Private Businesses

Another option in this cost consideration is to have resources and technology donated and/or offered at low-cost by corporations and private entities that are interested in making meaningful contributions to society. One of the things that I discuss later is partnerships, collaborations and cooperation, each of which will be necessary to hedge the success of the shift towards integrating AI technology into special education classrooms. In discussing these relationships, I go into greater detail about the need to partner and develop collaborations with AI technology corporations that can donate to and subsidize schools' and families' efforts to gain access to the AI technology tools and resources they need.

Before you completely dismiss this option as improbable and unrealistic, consider that corporate social responsibility (CSR), which represent an organization's discretionary actions, policies, and programs that appear to advance societal well-being in ways that extend beyond its immediate financial interests and the requirements of law,[82] lead companies to spend a significant amount of money on these activities each year. Some firms use CSR activities to focus on philanthropy; others utilize CSR opportunities to improve their operational effectiveness. However, I would like to make the case to corporations, as well as to the special education community, that there is an unrealized opportunity to consider special education as a potential target of corporations' and private businesses' corporate social responsibility initiatives. The needs of the CD community, which I have already discussed extensively, are clear, making it a worthy recipient of receiving CSR funds that corporations earmark to make a difference in society among those in need. When such investments are made into the CD community, the social benefits are reaped by us all, not just individuals in the CD community.

Let's take a moment to consider the benefits that corporations and private businesses could potentially experience if they choose to make the CD community recipients of their CSR funding. Consumers take into consideration firms' corporate social responsibility activities when making purchase decisions. In doing so, consumers may either increase their purchase intention or even pay higher prices for the firms' products and services if they consider the causes that the firms support through their CSR activities to be worthy causes.[83] Also, consumers often prefer to donate to a public cause through their purchase of private goods that are linked to the cause rather than donating directly to the cause as an individual, preferring to take such action so that their donation does not become visible.[84] As a result, through corporate efforts, consumers are able to see their donations at work benefiting society. For corporations, CSR activities have positive influences on brand and company evaluations, brand choice, brand recommendations, customer satisfaction and loyalty, customer-firm identification, and consumers' attributions in a product-harm crisis situation.[85]

Although it might seem counterintuitive, studies show that it is profitable for firms to donate a part of their profits to a charitable cause.[86] CSR investment into the CD community for the purpose of funding technology in special education classrooms is a valuable opportunity for corporations of any industry. If your corporation specializes in AI technology, great! You have a direct link to provide technology to the CD community and possibly even use research on this community to improve your products while making them recipients of your CSR activities.

If your company is outside of the technology industry, you can still benefit from investing into this community through CSR; research is clear that philanthropic activities can have a positive impact on a corporation's bottom line.

Almost everyone can think of corporations whose CSR targets environmental causes and organizations as recipients of their support. However, can you think of even one corporation that is a leader in supporting AI technology in special education classrooms? My guess is that you cannot. The closest type of relationship of this nature that readily comes to mind is that of grocery stores that donate a portion of their profits to schools, but this is still a far cry from the level of funding to integrate AI technology into special education classrooms. Thus, there is a considerable gap between need and potential opportunity in regard to CSR support of the CD community.

The first corporations and businesses that develop CSR strategies supporting AI in special education classrooms stand to reap significant benefits as an industry leader. Research also indicates that a corporation that is a first mover in setting CSR strategy has a competitive advantage over its competitors, and as a first mover, the corporation's profits are higher when consumers are made aware of CSR initiatives through marketing and communication. CSR helps corporations to be seen as industry leaders,[87] and with a sustainable CSR strategy, the first movers can achieve higher market share.[88]

Risk accumulates for corporations that do not have CSR strategies.[89] I urge corporations that do not have a CSR strategy or that want to distinguish themselves from other corporations who target their CSR activities to the same causes as the rest of the corporate crowd to consider selecting special education and the support of AI technology in special education classrooms, in particular, as the target of their CSR activities and investments.

Consider that by supporting AI in schools, you are changing the lives of individuals - individuals with fascinating stories who matter in society. In supporting the disability community through CSR, your corporation would also be tapping into one of the strongest and most loyal communities on the planet. In today's marketplace, is it important for firms to beat their rivals, not only by sales, but by implementing worthy CSR strategies and amplifying consumer sensitivity to the corporation's deeds and community actions through their marketing and communication strategies. Thus, it's not only important to have a CSR strategy in place but to ensure that it is targeted towards the support of a cause that people value and that this support is effectively communicated in such a way that it will influence the firm's bottom line: profit. Targeting the CD community for CSR investment is a great fit for companies seeking to accomplish these objectives.

The CD community, particularly funding AI technology for special education classrooms, is an untapped treasure for corporations and private businesses seeking to make a difference in our society through CSR investments for myriad reasons. The assistance is greatly needed in school classrooms, it improves the lives of children in need, and entities behind the CSR investments benefit from their activities by seeing value driven to their bottom line. Thus, CD-targeted CSR is a win for everyone; it just takes consideration of the CD community as an important and valuable part of our society rather than one to be overlooked to begin the worthwhile activity of investing in it!

State & Local Level Proposal 5: Crowdfunding

An additional option for funding for AI technology at the local level, one that may be particularly helpful for smaller funding projects at the district or school level, is crowdfunding.

Crowdfunding is an open call for money from the public. It has become an important source of funding for entrepreneurial, artistic, and social projects.[90] Successful crowdfunding projects are more likely to be projects that have non-profit goals, and the non-profit arena of education is an area where crowdfunding has had some success.[91] However, launching an effective crowdfunding campaign is not a simple and easy task. Successful crowdfunding efforts require attention to what information is presented to the public, how it is presented and how the creators of the fund interact with the crowd.[92] In order to be effective in crowdfunding efforts to raise funds for AI technology for students with CD, organizers will need to tell a compelling story. To accomplish this, they might, for example, choose to communicate the story in visual form, including photos and videos that showcase the progress students with CD have achieved through the use of technology.[93] The story of students with CD is a compelling one, just waiting to be told. When communicated in an effective manner, their stories will no doubt touch the hearts of people who will see their value and be willing to invest in their future.

Start with What You Have in Hand

Our pedagogy does not have to remain stagnant while we are waiting for all of the cost details to be fleshed out. In the meantime, while these discussions are taking place, there are some AI technology augmentations that we can begin using in the classroom as soon as tomorrow by using resources that are already available and that require little to no substantial investment from schools or families of students with CD. The fact that these tools and resources are already accessible means that we do not have to jump any cost hurdles in order to implement their use, making implementation relatively easy.

For example, we could start right now with allowing students with CD to use calculators to solve math problems. Almost everyone has an actual calculator or a calculator on their phone. If students possess neither, their parents can likely pick up one for less than a dollar at the nearest dollar store.

We could also normalize allowing students with CD to use their mobile devices to find answers on the internet to the teacher's questions. Again, there is unlikely to be a cost hurdle here, because most people, from toddlers on up, have access to a phone or tablet that they use to play games, watch videos, access the internet, etc.

While the integration of these tools and resources into the special education classroom might not come without a financial cost, they will come with a perception cost. We must be able to integrate their use in the instructional cycle to augment the education of students with CD without people viewing the use of these tools as "cheating" or "unfair." We could help people understand that it's simply a different way of looking at instruction in order to optimize the educational outcomes of special education students.

Innovate the Use of Your Existing Software

A lot of the implementation that can take place in the immediate future while leaders are fleshing out details about policies, cost, and curriculum is not dependent on expensive hardware. In many cases, all it takes is using the hardware that students already have access to and integrating the use of software that the school has available to improve the educational and post-educational outcomes of a student with CD. Take an inventory of the software the school already has and determine how students with CD can use it to access the information they need in each of their subject areas. For example, there might be software that can be loaded on the computers in the classroom that students can be permitted to use during lessons and during test taking, allowing them to access the information and answers they need. If, after you inventory your school's existing software, you determine that another type of software is needed to help special education students access the information they need efficiently and effectively, purchase the additional software. This will be significantly less expensive than waiting on the monies that are needed to purchase new hardware, and it can be implemented years sooner than the time it will take to work through all of the policy and cost considerations.

Another option is to make use of apps that students can load onto their phones and tablets. There's a whole host of apps that have been developed to assist people with cognitive disabilities in their functioning. The problem is that they are generally not allowed by teachers for use in the classroom. Granting special education students with permission to use these apps to augment their learning and access the information and answers they need is another way of using the software we currently have access to in a more efficient manner. It allows us to see immediate implementation without having to go out and buy costly new hardware or equipment, so the change is more like a subtle shift than a radical disruption. It's the best way of maximizing what we have and what we can gain access to for little to no cost, making implementation much more feasible and immediate.

An extended benefit of this option is that when we teach special education students how to access the software and apps they need in order to function at a higher level on their phones and tablets, their access to the information they need does not end at school; it follows them home. While they are taught to use the software at school, the benefits of what they learn in the classroom follow them 24 hours a day, from the bus, to stores, to restaurants, and anyplace else they go where they need to access information in order to function independently.

-app for early development
-small games
-data & stats output
-frozen screen ; iparent
-unlock parent

KADISHA AND ERIN'S STORY

Kadisha and Erin are best friends and currently attend Phoenix High School. Kadisha has a severe cognitive disability, and Erin has a mild cognitive disability. Their parents elected to augment their education with AI. Although Kadisha has a severe disability, she will graduate from high school performing at a 10th-grade level with the assistance of AI. Kadisha is excited about going to college. She has learned how to maximize the use of AI in her learning. Erin excelled in her studies and was selected as the valedictorian of her class. She was ecstatic about her selection as valedictorian. However, Erin's joy was short-lived; a small but vocal set of parents in the school felt that Erin's selection as valedictorian was not fair to kids without disabilities. Weeks before graduation, a petition started in school to have her selection as valedictorian revoked. It received 325 signatures in a school of 2,500 students, a mere 13% of the student body. Erin gave her valedictorian speech. A majority of the students and parents recognized her hard work and did not consider her a soulless robot. Erin even took a couple of minutes to recognize Kadisha in her speech. Although Kadisha was not at the top of the entire class, she ranked at the top of her cohort of students with severe cognitive disabilities. There is no category for that, so Erin wanted to recognize and honor her best friend, Kadisha.

This is the power of AI in education.

FEAR

Dismantling Fears of a Future Powered by AI

There is always a sense of intimidation surrounding shifts that take place in an environment; people are naturally fearful of the future when what lies ahead is unknown. The current narrative is that if we continue to build computers with human-level intellectual capacity, they are going to somehow multiply and take over the world. *How did such a narrative develop?* you might wonder. I attribute its development to a few things. First, there's the action sci-fi genre of movies that weave fictional plots about scientists building computer robots with such high levels of artificial intelligence that the robots become too smart for the scientists to control. Ultimately, the robots get together and hatch a plan to take over the world, and it's up to the action hero to foil their plan and save the world from robot domination. Even though these are clearly fantasy narratives that are meant purely for entertainment purposes, movie consumers tend to project them as realistic potentials of what could happen in the future... that is, if we don't stop AI development in its tracks and put some limits on how smart scientists are able to make robots.

The second factor that has contributed to the development of the "computers and robots are going to take over the world" narrative is the ways in which our lives are becoming increasingly dominated by technology. We all like technology. We like to have the latest phone and the latest features on those phones. We like to have the biggest, flattest, sharpest televisions that are currently on the market. We like to get our hands on the fastest, lightest laptops that can execute our commands with as little effort as possible on our part. We like to have homes that are so filled with digital features that they are smart: smart kitchen appliances, smart thermostats, smart electrical outlets that can turn the lights on and off, smart personal assistants... smart everything! Just a few years ago, our homes and lives were nowhere near as digitized as they are now. Thus, people look at how much technology has taken over their own lives and begin to project that at the rate technology is infiltrating their own lives, it could potentially take over the world in a matter of years, maybe even a decade or two. This scares them.

Then, there's the real-life scientific factor, which is grounded in a concept known as Moore's Law. According to Moore's Law, which was created based on an insightful prediction by computer engineer and Intel Corporation co-founder Gordon E. Moore around 1970, "...processor speeds, or overall processing power for computers, will double every two years." Over the years, computer companies have found that Moore's speculation of what the future would hold for computer processing power to be unfounded. Despite the clear evidence to the contrary, however, many have subscribed to the law as truth, allowing it to serve as the benchmark for rates of innovation in the computer industry.[94] Thus, 50 years after the law became the "golden rule for the electronics industry and a springboard for innovation," Moore's insights continue to influence the development of smaller, faster, and more affordable technology at exponential speeds, resulting in a more widespread use of digital technology and personal electronics that have been seamlessly integrated into our daily lives.[95]

Like anything else in life, the development that Moore's Law has inspired over the past several decades has both its pros and cons. According to Intel Corporation:

> This vision of an endlessly empowered and interconnected future brings clear challenges and benefits. Privacy and evolving security threats are persistent and growing concerns. But the benefits of ever smarter, ubiquitous computing technology, learning to anticipate our needs, can help keep us healthier, safer, and more productive in the long run.[96]

As you can see, Intel acknowledges both the benefits and potential drawbacks of technological innovation. However, as you can also see, they choose to place greater focus on the benefits rather than the potential threats. I'm with them. When it's all said and done, the benefits to how an increased use and dependence upon technology can enhance our lives far outweigh the potential threats. I'm not saying to blindly ignore the potential threats as though they do not exist; this is not what Intel is saying either. Instead, what we're both saying is that we should give greater weight to the benefits that technology innovations can offer while simultaneously mitigating any potential threats regarding privacy, security and other challenges.

Unfortunately, people who engage in anti-technology mania allow the potential threats to privacy and security – unquestionably, very *real* threats – to overshadow the benefits that technology stands to introduce into our daily lives. Anyone can see that the innovation and development of technology is occurring right before our very eyes at an unbelievable pace. Every day, we see headlines flashing across our phones, televisions and computers introducing the latest and greatest new technological developments, many of which we once thought never to be humanly possible to develop. I acknowledge that seeing once-unimaginable things brought to life and seeing change occur so rapidly can be intimidating. It can be particularly disturbing for people who tend to be averse to change. If you're one of these people, please rest assured that computers and robots are not going to take over the world. If we succeed in normalizing the dependence and constant reliance on AI technology for students with CD in special education classrooms, the benefits are going to completely eclipse the potential challenges. You'll see.

> **...we can't just ignore people's fears about integrating AI technology into classrooms; we must proactively address them in order to prevent subversion, sabotage, half-hearted implementation and low morale regarding our efforts toward making the shift.**

You might wonder why I'm even taking the time to address the fear of computers and robots taking over the world in the first place. The reason I'm speaking to these concerns is that if they go unaddressed, they can produce resistance – conscious or subconscious – to the adoption and implementation of new processes in an organization. In our case, people driven by such fears could be our most vocal and passionate opponents as we seek to shift the pedagogy of special education classrooms by normalizing a dependence on AI technology. Because of this, we can't just ignore people's fears about integrating AI technology into classrooms; we must proactively address them in order to prevent subversion, sabotage, half-hearted implementation and low morale regarding our efforts toward making the shift.

What to Do If You're Fearful of AI Technology

The reality is that technology is here to stay, and its use will increase as we move into the future. If you are afraid of technology, no amount of telling you not to fear technology is going to make you feel better. Rather than give in to fear, I urge you to channel that fear into something productive like engaging in critical discussions about how we use technology to improve our lives and how we manage that technology safely. Fear is a natural response to the unknown and serves an important function: it should alert us, the human race, to the potential dangers of technology and spur us into preventative action. What we should not do when we feel a sense of fear about technology is allow it to stop our technological process or to make us advocate becoming luddites (a term used to describe individuals opposed to new technology, derived from early 19th century textile workers who destroyed machines in wool and cotton mills because they feared losing their jobs to the machines). Technology and robots might replace quite a few jobs in the global workforce because of their efficiency and ability to operate with precision, but with dedicated effort and attention, we can manage the potentials of this technology. We must also consider the reality that although technology and robots will change the job landscape in the future, it will also create new jobs we never imagined.

"How can you say this so indefinitely?" you might ask. According to Harvard University AI expert, Dr. Mark Esposito, in every industry where AI is used, the aim is not to displace human resources who work in these industries, but to improve society. He explains, "To ease fears over job loss... business owners can frame the conversation around creating new, more functional jobs. As technologies improve efficiencies and create new insights, new jobs that build on those improvements are sure to arise."[97] He further asserts that when we understand the things we can do and how we can do these things with greater levels of accuracy, efficiency, and effectiveness, jobs are created.

Then, in response to the fears that robots with AI functioning could one day begin operating independently of their human creators and potentially take over the world, Dr. Esposito explains the responsibility of developers to create AI to create probabilistic rather than deterministic AI technology. Probabilistic AI predicts the likelihood of something occurring based on the data and then offers a recommendation to its human user to make the decision, taking into account considerations that cannot necessarily be quantified by data. Deterministic AI would make the decision on its own without regard to any uncertainties. According to Esposito, "There needs to be cooperation between machines and people... but we will never invite machines to make a decision on behalf of people."[98]

Instead of focusing on the potential of AI to take over society, cause massive job loss and potentially make us their subjects, I prefer to focus on the potential vast benefits of AI for the humans who need it the most in our society. When we focus our energies in this direction, AI technology is not something to be feared but something to be embraced. In fact, a focus on human need and how there is a solution that now exists is what sparked my interest in this project.

Common Concerns of Critics Against the Use of AI in Educating Students with CD

Allow me to address some of the most common concerns I've heard surrounding the pedagogical shift towards integrating AI technology into special education classrooms. Using AI will not...

- **Result in the physical underdevelopment or deterioration of students with CD brains.**

  People wear glasses to augment their vision deficiencies, and this does not make their eyes weaker; it just helps them to function as close to normal as possible. Physically disabled people use wheelchairs to augment their physical deficiencies, and this does not make their legs weaker; they just help them to function in as close to a normal way as possible. In the same way, using AI to augment learning deficiencies will not make cognition weaker; it will simply help the cognitively disabled function as close to normal as possible.

- **Cripple the potential intellectual development of students with CD or hinder their ability to think on their own when their AI technology is not accessible.**

  These students' intellectual development or intrinsic thinking capacities will not be hindered any more than they would be if they did not use AI technology.

- **Result in an over-reliance on technology among students with CD so much so that they cannot function socially.**

  Keep in mind that with the shift I am proposing, a heavy use or dependence on technology will not occur in pre-school or elementary school, which is when children are socialized and their skills to interact with others in a socially-appropriate manner are formed. Their heavy dependence on technology, which I propose will not come until the middle and high school years, will not hinder them from functioning socially; it will increase their social confidence, enthusiasm about school, and their peer interactions, because they will feel better about themselves and their ability to function like their peers through the use of AI.

- **Produce screen-addicted students with CD whose eyes and fingers are focused on their phones all day long.**

Much of the AI that has already been prototyped and that is currently under development is hands-free and screen-free. Even if students do use their phones to access the technology, they will likely be doing so in order to aid their basic functioning. Students with CD who depend heavily on technology to function will likely use no more screen time than the average student without a disability who spends excessive hours each day on their phones, scrolling through social media and watching videos on the internet.

- **Create a big gap between the haves who can afford all of the latest technology and the have-nots who cannot afford the latest technology.**

The shift that I am proposing is one that is grounded in a rationale of equity. Every school system will receive the resources that it needs to provide AI tools and resources to their students, because these resources will be distributed equitably.

- **Produce a population of students with CD who are "smarter" than students without disabilities.**

Students with CD will not rely on technology to become smarter than their non-disabled counterparts. Remember,

AI does not produce geniuses; it gives individuals with mental deficiencies the ability to function on par with their non-disabled peers.

- **Eliminate the need for teachers in the classroom or result in the loss of jobs.**

There will never be a time when teachers are no longer necessary in the classroom because of students' dependence on technology to increase their educational outcomes. Teachers will always be necessary to provide the instruction the students need as well as the psychological and emotional support they need to be successful in learning.

- **Require new certifications for schoolteachers that are AI-specific.**

While this will be a policy discussion, it is highly unlikely that teachers will be required to get new certifications before they can continue teaching students with CD. I do anticipate a new certification that teachers can pursue that trains them as specialists in AI-augmented learning, as having specialists of this type in a school will help to optimize instruction of students with CD. However, this new certification will be voluntary.

- **Bankrupt the school system through the purchase of thousands of state-of-the-art gadgets for each student.**

One of the things that I am proposing to hedge the success of the shift towards AI-augmented learning is the donation of AI technology tools and resources by technology companies to schools. Additionally, I anticipate federal funding being allowed to be allocated towards the purchase of tools and resources necessary for the successful implementation and sustainability of AI-augmented learning programs.

- **Throw the world into chaos overnight.**

    Nothing about a "shift" in the instructional cycle of students with CD will throw the world into chaos. Further, the shift is not one that will take place overnight; implementation will be gradual.

A Final Appeal Against Anti-technology Attitudes

Let me help to calm the general sense of paranoia that threatens to arise based on how people anticipate AI-augmented learning will drastically change the world as we know it. First, technology is not making us weaker as a human race by diminishing our mental faculties and under-development of our brains. Instead, quite the opposite occurs when we use technology as an extension of our intelligence. Our ability to manipulate AI technology and use it astutely makes us sharper, keener, and more intelligent. Overall, the combined benefits of AI-augmented learning will improve outcomes for all of us.

Next, although technology might not be a choice for everyone – everyone might not want or need it – it should at least be presented as an option based on the wide range of benefits it offers to the lives of students with CD. None of this is being forced on anyone who doesn't need it. Allow the policymakers, educators, parents, and students to look at all of the research, discuss all the options, and decide for themselves whether or not AI-augmented learning should be available in the classroom. Don't take that freedom of choice away from them by campaigning against a reliance on technology, grounded in a fear of the unknown. We already know the educational and post-educational outcomes of students with CD who don't use AI technology in their instructional cycle. How about allowing these students to explore the outer limits of what is possible if they do use AI technology in their learning. How about letting them choose to do something new?

Then, we've got to get our perspective right about how AI will ultimately affect education. Although schools have technology in their classrooms and sitting on the shelves of their resource rooms, they intentionally limit students' use of it. Teachers may allow students to use technology as supplements, as long as these supplements do not replace the students' abilities to perform on their own the same functions that the technology performs for them. That is, they can engage in limited use of technology as long as they don't become dependent on them. What I'm proposing is a shift towards the deliberate, intentional and unrestricted use of this technology that actually encourages a dependence on it among students with CD. Augmenting their learning through the use of AI technology will not only improve the overall impact of their education but also improve their overall quality of life after graduation, resulting in their ability to live self-sufficient, independent lives. How could anyone say "No" to such amazing opportunities that AI technology can offer to the lives of the people who stand to benefit from it the most?

There will always be some anti-technology people on the other side of the aisle who believe that technology is dangerous and that it will take over the world if we allow it to pervade every aspect of our lives. They couch their resistance to allowing students with CD to augment learning with AI technology in the classroom based on the argument that it is just too much technology. However, it is funny that they don't say it's just too much technology when it's being used for their own benefit. They have smart phones, smart TVs, smart radios in their cars, smart watches, and a host of gadgets and devices that are considered AI technology. Not only do they possess these technologies; they live by them. Without access to them daily, these people would be lost! It is selfish on our part to use technology for our own benefit but deny technology for people who actually need it to survive, improve their lives, and prosper.

ALINA'S STORY

Alina is headed to her college counselor's office to discuss her college classes. It is Alina's second week on campus. As she walks toward her counselor's office, she briefly thinks of the hard work she has had to put in academically and socially just to get into college. She also thinks back to when she first started in elementary school with AI-augmented education. In 2021, the smallest commonplace computer was a handheld phone. Now, her computer is the size of a one-inch square, and it is integrated into her clothing. Alina has a moderate cognitive disability and has mastered augmenting her learning with AI. An earpiece, her computer, and a watch are the main technology devices she uses to augment her everyday functioning. Her technology support is invisible. With practice, over time, and by learning the unique characteristics of her disability, Alina has become a competent learner. As an adult, her technology is like a favorite pair of shoes, just right and comfortable in every situation. As Alina walks into her counselor's office, he says, "Welcome! Let's get started on your college future. I see that your transcript says that you graduated with a high school diploma that included AI augmentation. We require everyone, including students with CD, to achieve the same standards for graduation." Alina smiles and says, "I would have it no other way. Let's get started! I am ready. My college goals are only limited by my ambition."

**This is the power of
AI in education.**

PARTNERSHIPS, COLLABORATIONS & COOPERATION

Success of the AI-augmented Learning Shift

I have a vision for one of the most special and unique populations of individuals that I've ever had the privilege of working with in my life: special education students. My vision is that AI is included in the instructional cycle for children with CD so that they have educational and post-educational outcomes that meet or exceed the outcomes of their peers. I envision students with CD graduating with high school diplomas that indicate that they meet the same standards as their non-disabled peers. I dream that these amazing students will move on to post-secondary education and have access to the same employment and earning potential over the course of their lives as their non-disabled peers. I envision these capable individuals being trained to use technology to develop such a strong command of information that they are able to use it in any context to solve problems. I envision that, because they were taught in school to effectively lean on technology to augment their cognitive shortcomings, they are able to demonstrate mastery of information in any real life setting. Finally, I envision individuals with CD living self-sufficient, independent, and healthy lives in which they thrive rather than merely survive. This vision is what drives my passionate advocacy for a shift in special education pedagogy to include AI-technology augmented learning.

> **"**
>
> I envision individuals with CD living self-sufficient, independent, and healthy lives in which they thrive rather than merely survive.
>
> This vision is what drives my passionate advocacy...
>
> **"**

Strategic Alliances Necessary to Hedge the Success of the AI in CD Shift

No shift proposal of this magnitude would be complete without the introduction of some actionable steps. There are many parts to the shift, all of which need to participate in order to guarantee its success. Partnerships, collaborations and cooperation will be essential in making AI-augmented learning and technology-dependent functioning a normalized part of life for individuals with cognitive disabilities.

1 | Corporations

The first set of players that we must build a partnership with to hedge the success of the shift are corporations in the technology industry. Ensuring the cooperation of the technology companies at the forefront of developing AI is a fundamental prerequisite to the successful development of programs that can effectively integrate AI into the instructional cycle of special education classrooms. I anticipate that positioning themselves at the forefront of AI/CD program development will be an attractive proposition for the technology industry for a number of reasons. First and foremost is the unparalleled opportunity for challenge within the space of the current innovations that are occurring in AI, which I previously discussed.

Current work in the AI space is centered on being the first to develop a computer that thinks and processes like the human mind, at or above the average level of human intelligence. What I am proposing is a parallel track of AI that is much more challenging and innovative – computer programs that can take on the unique thinking and processing challenges that those with cognitive disabilities face. This type of AI development, which is situated on the more complex terrain of thought augmentation, is the kind of expansion in AI research that will directly benefit those in the CD community, both students and adults. If I know anything about people who work in innovation, it's that they are always intrigued by novel and complex challenges. If there never existed a novel and complex challenge before, there exists one now in trying to merge AI with CD.

It also goes without saying that these technology corporations should not try to develop these new technologies in a theoretical vacuum. Instead, they should precede their efforts by retaining a subject matter expert, a consultant who specializes in AI in CD. Having an expert on hand is necessary to help technology companies to better understand how they can best support the development and adaptation of their technologies in a school setting. After all, very few techies have ever worked in an educational space, so having someone on-hand that can explain the critical intersections between AI and education is a necessary requirement. An educational consultant can also shed additional light on grade-level differences, socioeconomic considerations, and other nuances that affect educational attainment that might never come to the mind of an AI developer. Then, after the development of the technology, the expert consultant can lead the companies in testing them in real-life classroom situations, overseeing the testing for maximum optimization in special education classrooms. In fact, teachers and students with CD could be used in every phase of development of the technology, including prototyping, pilot testing and refinement.

Armed with an awareness that most school systems have more goals and objectives than they are able to finance with the tax dollars they are given each year, it is my hope that the technology industry would subsidize or share the costs with the school systems for the development of AI technology. Even better, these companies could make donations of the AI technology to the school systems outright and even couple these material donations with financial grants so that all of the schools in the systems could have access to the equipment and software they need for their special education classrooms. Then, once these innovations are mass produced, they can be targeted to the market of individuals who do not have cognitive disabilities but who might benefit from such augmentations, nonetheless, and thus recover a portion of their profits. One common example of such a technology is speech recognition software. While this technology benefits individuals with disabilities, its inclusion in everyday products like mobile phones, computers, voice-controlled personal assistants, smart speakers, etc. is a source of profit. As new technology is developed to assist students with CD, there will be other opportunities for mass profit among the larger population. Students with CD are people, and what benefits one individual with adjustment can benefit everyone with convenience and efficiency.

Then, there's the opportunity for companies working in the AI industry to simply help a population in need that rarely has the resources to help itself. The return on such a socially-responsible undertaking: good feelings. Knowing that you're not simply "helping people" but literally changing lives, giving an entire community a chance to live and function in unprecedented ways that opens up a whole new world of opportunities before them, has to stand for something, right? My admonition would be for technology companies that work in the AI space and that are looking for a way to give back to society seriously consider adopting the CD community with the aim of helping to mitigate the challenges that hinder them from living self-sufficient, independent lives.

Finally, I'm aware that that the technology industry is not a social service industry; it is a revenue-generating, profit-conscious collection of organizations singularly focused on driving value to the bottom line. In other words, people are in the technology industry to make money. I get it. Fortunately, there is vast profit potential in developing software and technologies that can not only be used in school classrooms, but it can be marketed to school-age students and their parents, and to adults in the public. More than 10 percent of Americans have a cognitive disability and can benefit from technologies that augment their day-to-day functioning, from intermediate and high school, to college, to the workplace. With the proper technological support, this population of adults can increase their abilities to function and operate with greater levels of self-sufficiency. Thus, what the potential opportunity to undertake a new challenge and the social benefits cannot do to move those in technology towards embracing the development of AI for CD, the profit potential should.

2 | Community

Next, collaborations in the community between education institutions and corporations will be necessary to hedge the success of the shift towards AI-augmented learning. They say that "teamwork makes the dream work," and this could be no truer when examining how collaborations in the community can aid the development, implementation and sustainability of AI technology into special education classrooms. Community collaborations are critical in hedging the success of the shift. If you are a part of a community that is interested in advancing such an initiative, I recommend working with the key players in your community to assemble a discovery team. The purpose of the discovery team is to ask and answer questions about how the innovation will be brought to life, how and what resources are needed to make it a reality, who's going to be a part of the team and what role they are going to play, what resources will be required, what AI in CD classrooms will look like in the community, where and when the testing of the innovation will occur, and all of the other practical ins and outs.

Who will be on the discovery team will be just as important as what the discovery team does. For beginners, in the same way that I recommended retaining a subject matter expert, an AI in CD expert consultant to lead technology companies in their efforts to develop technologies for special education classrooms, I also recommend that the same type of expert consultant be included on your discovery team. Without someone trained, skilled, experienced, and fully-immersed in the research to guide your discovery team, your team could end up doing a lot of work and making a lot of progress but in the wrong direction.

Your AI/CD consultant will keep you on the right path, operating with the most recent research findings and strategies, and ensure that you are operating effectively and efficiently. Then, you'll need to ensure that you have some other key players on your team like special education teachers, representatives from the school system, representatives of local technology corporations that will lead the AI development, key community influencers (the ones that can open doors and make introductions), and even a few special education students (representing different grade levels).

3 | Special Education Associations

Finally, collaborations and cooperation with special education associations will be necessary to hedge the success of the shift towards AI-augmented learning. These national associations normally have a mission advocating for the needs of special education students in some way, so they would be the perfect partners in our efforts to promote the use of AI technology in enhancing the learning outcomes of students with CD. These associations have the power to reach massive numbers of our core constituency, families with children with cognitive disabilities, through conferences, newsletters, email blasts, mailouts, and other forms of communication. If we can partner with them, they can instantly spread the message about the shift we are advocating to millions of people, providing educational materials that build awareness and that provide instruction to these families about what they can do to influence the policymakers in their areas to adopt AI-augmented learning for students with CD.

Specific Actions for Audiences on a Local Level

Parents

If you are a parent, now that you have achieved a higher awareness of the topic that is on the table and its endless potentials, it's time to take specific action. Write letters to your school board about the need for AI in classrooms for students with CD. Write letters to your congressmen asking them how we can incorporate these ideas into law. Make phone calls to the school and school system asking them if they've heard about and considered the potentials of incorporating AI into classrooms and advocating for AI in CD classrooms. Add your signature to circulating petitions and even begin petitions of your own insisting that school systems, school boards and political decisionmakers require the use of AI in special education classrooms. Be like that squeaky wheel that refuses to remain quiet until it is addressed to its satisfaction. This is the only way to ensure that your voice gets heard and your concerns get addressed regarding matters of education in the school system. It's these kinds of grassroot efforts that ultimately end up affecting change in our society!

Teachers

If you are a teacher who is reading this book, I have little doubt that you now clearly understand the leaps and bounds of progress that students with CD can make through the use of AI-augmented learning. When society looks at how much students have been able to learn in a classroom, everyone looks at the teacher; he or she is a "good teacher" if students learn a lot and have good educational outcomes, and he or she is a "bad teacher" if students do not succeed in learning and have poor educational outcomes. Because of this unique position, you have a voice like no other group involved in this debate, because you are the one held responsible for the learning outcomes of students in the classroom. Thus, the first action I encourage you to take is that of using your voice! Begin talking about the potentials of how AI technology can help to augment the learning of students with CD, whether these are the students you teach or not. People will listen closely to what you have to say, because as a teacher, you have the most credible and trustworthy perspective about whether AI augmentation should be integrated into the learning cycle or not. Simply start talking!

Raise awareness about the potential benefits of using AI for students with CD in special education classrooms. Educate yourself to an even greater degree about AI-augmented learning, and if you have the ability to do so, offer this education to others. Host a mini-presentation for other teachers in the teachers' lounge. Host an afternoon or evening workshop in a meeting room for parents of students with CD that teaches them about the significant impact the technology can have on their children's learning outcomes so that you can turn them into advocates, too. Then, use your influence as a teacher to write letters to the district, state and regional officials who make the policy decisions that will ultimately determine whether or not the shift towards AI-augmented learning will become a part of the instructional cycle for students with CD. Whatever you do, don't diminish the powerful influence you have as a teacher to advocate for this cause and make a difference!

Administrators and Policy Makers

The very first conversations that must occur if actions are to be taken to integrate AI into the CD instructional cycle will be held on a policy level by policymakers, because adopting this innovative, new approach will undoubtedly have significant policy implications. Typically, policymakers have the exclusive authority to give the green light that school systems and districts need to move forward with engagement of a major new initiative. Without policymakers giving their stamp of permissibility for the systematic, programmatic use of AI in special education classrooms, the whole discussion will be dead in the water. In addition to granting permission to school systems and districts to engage the use of AI as a strategy, those at the policymaking level also have the power to smooth the way, removing any constraints that might hinder the implementation of the new programs in schools. In fact, when I consider how much of a role policymakers play in paving the way for school systems and districts to embrace the use of AI in CD classrooms, it's safe to say that the whole approach, from implementation to sustainability, rises and falls on their understanding and acceptance of the potential benefits of using AI in CD classrooms.

That said, before we consider bombarding policymakers with our petitions and demands for adopting this new approach to meeting the needs of special education students, we must be first committed to educating them, raising awareness about the benefits of AI in CD classrooms. I am fully confident that with a clearly laid-out, well-informed presentation of the proposed who, what, where, when, how, and why they should get behind the novel idea, there's no way they can say no. Consider yourself. After reading this book and the arguments that I have extended in it, I'm confident that I've made a believer out of you (I could be wrong... if I am, just humor me). The same is true for the policymakers who are also the keyholders to opening the doors that need to swing open for school systems and districts to begin conversations about how to systematically implement AI-based initiatives into their special education programs. If we take the time to show them the benefits and great potential that lies in fully embracing AI as a means to enhance how we serve special education students, they will become enthusiastic advocates, too.

After policymakers open the door, the ball will leave their court and fall into those responsible for picking up the conversation and running with it: school systems and districts. Believe it or not, in most cases, the biggest bang for the buck in conversations about incorporating AI into classrooms for students with CD, particularly matters of engagement and implementation, will occur at the district level (and in some cases, this will also include the school level). If you work as a district-level administrator, you must understand that before the other players in administration will even consider integrating AI into CD classrooms, they are going to need help understanding the concept. Thus, before there can be an implementation phase, there must first be an education phase.

During this phase, you carry the weighty responsibility of helping to introduce the concept to administrators and offering your recommendations about how to implement it. You have a prime opportunity to initiate dialogue within your school system about how AI can be integrated into CD learning environments, what it will look like, how it will potentially impact the current learning environment, how it might impact the district's budget, what policies and procedures need to be put into place that do not already exist, what structural components are needed to support the introduction of AI into CD classrooms, and more. Further, on the district level, administrators have the ability to bring parents of students with CD into these discussions – a member-checking of sorts – in order to ensure that whatever strategies are put into place by the district resonate with what they know to be the needs of their children. One of the most compelling tools that you can use to persuade each of these audiences over to becoming advocates of AI in CD classrooms: a model demonstration. Work with local technology companies engaged in AI development to create a software prototype or demo of what the technology looks like in action. It will speak volumes to compel them to embrace AI in CD classrooms in ways that your mere words cannot.

Once the district adopts the idea of integrating AI into CD classrooms, there are some additional practical steps administrators can take to ensure that the initiative advances beyond a conversation, that it results in action. For example, one of the first steps that school districts will need to take is to educate the educators, or the classroom teachers, about using AI in CD classrooms and how it can be included in curriculum opportunities throughout the educational life cycle. Encourage them to explore the opportunity and ask questions.

Additionally, district administrators can ensure that the topic of AI in special education is offered as a topic covered in continuing education workshops that are required for teachers to maintain their certifications. This will ensure that the topic remains top of mind for them and that they remain aware of the latest innovations and advancements of AI's use among individuals with CD that can be employed in their classrooms. Another practical step that administrators can take is to include presentations and roundtable discussions surrounding AI in education at annual conferences. Be sure to engage experts in the field, inviting them to present at these gatherings in order to ensure that the content presented is the most recent and cutting-edge. Doing so will further expose educators and administrators to the latest advancements of AI in CD and keep educators current with the potentials of what can be realized in their own school systems and classrooms. Finally – and this is my ultimate ideal – it would be great if a district administrator finished reading this book, received a transfer of my enthusiasm surrounding AI in CD, and introduced a program in which the district piloted an AI in CD program in an elementary, middle and high school in their district. That would be awesome.

Specific Actions for Audiences on a National Level

There is a lot that can be done on a national level to advance the agenda of incorporating AI into classrooms serving CD classrooms. For example, supporters who desire to make a national impact can develop non-profit associations that advocate for the use of AI in special education classrooms around the nation. These organizations should never operate in a vacuum. Rather, everything they do should include collaborations with local decision makers on how to develop, implement, and sustain the programs that they propose. Another specific action that can be undertaken on a national level is integrating discussions about AI in special education classrooms into national education conferences. This will not only introduce the concept, but it will help to keep AI in education at the forefront of conversations about the intersections between technology and education. Then, hosting national conferences that are specifically geared towards learning about AI in education would be ideal, especially if a cross-section of school districts could be represented at the gathering. Big, corporate events like conferences are wonderful vehicles for efficiently disseminating new information to interested audiences, vested players with a genuine interest in whatever theme is at the center of the gathering. Presenting keynotes and general sessions about what's new and relevant in the AI industry for school systems at events like these would be a beneficial move to advance our agenda.

Ultimately, we must all – at the very least – remain open to the potentials of what the educational and post-educational quality of life outcomes could be like for students with CD if we dared to incorporate AI technology into their instructional pedagogy. AI technology has already resulted in monumental advancements in practically every other industry in which it is used. What do you say to giving it a go in education to see what it can do when it's developed and tested to its very limits by the population that needs its intelligence the most – the CD community? We already know the learning outcomes and quality of life that result when we don't use such innovations in special education classrooms. How about we push the envelope together and go on a journey to discover what the learning outcomes could be if we make this pedagogical shift towards the use of AI technology?

To be on the side of keeping things the same or doing nothing to make a shift is an indication that you're fine with the outcomes that current special education pedagogy has produced for decades. However, aligning with us as an advocate for the shift towards AI says that you see the problem, you're not okay with the status quo, and you're willing to position yourself on the side of progress and innovation, if it will mean producing better educational and post-educational outcomes for people who are unable to advocate for themselves. I encourage you to partner with us and our equity-based education agenda today, or at the very least, allow others to move forward without your opposition, as we champion the adoption of AI-augmented learning for the benefit of students with CD and for the benefit of our entire society.

GLOSSARY OF TERMS

Adaptations – Changes in educational environments that allow students with disabilities to participate in inclusive environments by compensating for learners' weaknesses.[99]

Aptitude – Native or acquired characteristics that signify the ability for an individual to learn or increase competency in a designated area of study when provided with adequate training or education in that area.[100]

Artificial intelligence (AI) - A branch of computer science that aims to imbue software with the ability to analyze its environment using either predetermined rules and search algorithms, or pattern recognizing machine learning models, and then make decisions based on those analyses. Also known as machine intelligence.

Attention Deficit Disorder (ADD) – A term formerly used to describe the condition of individuals who are not significantly hyperactive or impulsive yet have difficulties paying attention. The more commonly-used synonym instead of ADD today is AD/HD.[101]

Attention Deficit/Hyperactivity Disorder (AD/HD) – A term used to describe the condition of individuals who are significantly hyperactive or impulsive, making it difficult for them to control their behavior, sit still and concentrate, or pay attention.[102]

Autism – A pervasive developmental disability that affects an individual's ability to communicate, both verbally and nonverbally, and that is characterized by a lack of ability to read, understand and interpret the emotions of others and by having difficulty with ordinary functioning in social environments, including a school setting.[103]

Cognitive development – The process of the brain creating internal mental structures that make it possible for an individual to think, reason, read, and learn, starting from birth. One of the primary goals of education is to create opportunities for the development of these abilities.[104]

Cognitive disability – An obstacle that an individual has in learning, which might include one or multiple challenges like understanding, processing, recognizing, perceiving, remembering, and choosing content or information. These difficulties can also include the lack of ability to focus for an extended amount of time in order to retain what they are taught.[105]

Dyslexia – A neurobiological learning disability that affects an individual's development in reading, writing and spelling skills (decoding and encoding), thus hindering the development of their literacy.[106]

Dementia – An umbrella term used to describe conditions and diseases characterized by deteriorating thinking, problem-solving and language skills, as well as memory loss, hindering an individual's ability to function and carry out routine daily activities. The most common cause of dementia is Alzheimer's disease.[107]

Down syndrome – A medical birth defect that occurs when a baby is born with an extra chromosome, which affects the baby's development, producing mental and physical challenges. These individuals often have a mildly-to-moderately low IQ and usually require extra assistance and help in school.[108]

Dyscalculia – A learning disorder that makes it difficult for individuals to engage in mathematical reasoning, computation, or any number-related task, despite receiving appropriate education, and regardless of intelligence level.[109]

Equality – The quality or state of being equal, as in of the same measure, quantity, amount, nature, or status; regarding or affecting all objects in the same way.[110]

Equity – A term used to describe justice, according to natural law or right, and dealing fairly and equally with all concerned.[111]

Fairness – The quality of operating with a lack of favoritism toward one side or another, or the quality or state of being marked by impartiality and honesty; freedom from self-interest and prejudice.[112]

Intellectual disability – A specific category of challenges to general cognitive functioning that result in a lower intelligence quotient (IQ) and introduce substantial challenges in how students' social skills and how they adapt to new contexts or situations. Formerly referred to as "mental retardation."[113]

Special education – Instruction that is specially designed to increase a student's chances for academic success.[114]

ENDNOTES

1   Monett, D., Lewis, C., & Thorisson, K. (2020). Introduction to the
    JAGI special issue "On defining artificial intelligence." *Journal of
    Artificial Intelligence*, 11(2), p. 1.

2   Wang, P. (2008). What do you mean by "AI"? In Wang, P., Goertzel, B.,
    and Franklin, S., eds., *Artificial General Intelligence 2008*. Proceedings
    of the First AGI Conference, Frontiers in Artificial Intelligence and
    Applications, 171. Amsterdam, The Netherlands: IOS Press. 362-373.

3   https://www.techopedia.com/definition/190/artificial-intelligence-ai

4   *Cognitive Disability vs. Intellectual Disability*. (2018, August 21).
    Retrieved from https://study.com/academy/lesson/cognitive-
    disability-vs-intellectual-disability.html.

5   American Association on Intellectual and Developmental Disabilities.
    (2019). *Frequently asked questions on intellectual disability*. Accessed
    February 28, 2020. https://www.aaidd.org/intellectual-disability/
    definition/faqs-on-intellectual-disability

6   *Cognitive Disability vs. Intellectual Disability*

7   *American Association on Intellectual and Developmental Disabilities*.

8   Ibid.

9   Patel, D., Apple, R., Kanungo, S., & Akkal, A. (2018). Intellectual
    disability: Definitions, evaluation, and principles of treatment.
    Pediatric Medicine, 1(11). doi: 10.21037/pm.2018.12.02

10 *Cognitive Disability vs. Intellectual Disability*.

11 Backer, T., & Howard, E. (2007). Cognitive impairments and the
    prevention of homelessness: Research and practice review. *The
    Journal of Primary Prevention*, 28, 375-388.

12 Ditchman N., Kosyluk K., Lee, E., & Jones N. (2016). How stigma
    affects the lives of people with intellectual disabilities: An overview.
    In: Scior K., Werner S. (eds) *Intellectual Disability and Stigma*.
    Palgrave Macmillan, London, pp. 31-47.

13 Tomasello, J., & Brand, B. (2018). *How ESSA and IDEA can
    support college and career readiness for students with disabilities:
    Considerations for states*. Washington, DC: American Institutes for
    Research Youth Policy Forum. Retrieved from https://files.eric.ed.gov/
    fulltext/ED586419.pdf

14 *Disability and economic status*. American Psychological Association.
    Accessed February 27, 2020.

15 Backer, T., & Howard, E. (2007). Cognitive impairments and the
    prevention of homelessness: Research and practice review. *The
    Journal of Primary Prevention*, 28, 375-388. https://link.springer.com/
    article/10.1007/s10935-007-0100-1

16   Ibid.
17   Anderson, C., Owens, L., & Nerlich, A. (2017). Poverty, disability, and vocational assessment of youth with disabilities. *VEWAA Journal*, 41(2), p. 4. https://projecte3.com/download/VEWAA-Journal-Special.pdf#page=7
18   *Disability and economic status.*
19   *Disability and economic status.*
20   Bollard, M., Mcleod, E., & Dolan, A. (2018). Exploring the impact of health inequalities on the health of adults with intellectual disability from their perspective. Disability & Society, 33(6). https://doi.org/10.1080/09687599.2018.1459476
21   Wakefield, K. (2020). Artificial intelligence in business. SAS. https://www.sas.com/en_gb/insights/articles/analytics/applications-of-artificial-intelligence.html
22   https://ai.google/social-good
23   Ibid.
24   Hilpinen, R. (1970). Knowing that one knows and the classical definition of knowledge. *Synthese*, 21(2), 109-132.
25   Knowledge. (n.d.). Merriam-Webster Online. In Merriam-Webster. Retrieved May 1, 2020, from http://www.merriam-webster.com/dictionary/equity.
26   Loveless, T. (2004). *Computation skills, calculators, and achievement gaps: An analysis of NAEP items.* Paper presented at the Annual Conference of the American Educational Research Association: San Diego, CA. Retrieved June 3, 2020 from https://www.brookings.edu/research/computation-skills-calculators-and-achievement-gaps-an-analysis-of-naep-items
27   Rubenstein, R. (2001). The impact of two standards-based mathematics curricula on student achievement in Massachusetts. *Journal of Research in Mathematics Education*, 32, 368-398.
28   Cockcroft, W. (1982). *Mathematics Counts: Report of the Committee of Inquiry into the teaching of mathematics in schools under the chairmanship of Dr. W.H. Cockcroft.* London: HMSO.
29   Ruthven, K. (1996). Calculators in the mathematics curriculum: The scope of personal computational technology. In *International handbook of mathematics education* (pp. 435–468). Dordrecht, The Netherlands: Kluwer Academic.
30   Planov, M., Baunder, D., Carr, D. & Sarrar, R. (1993). Structuring teachers' attitudinal changes: A follow-up study. Technology and Teacher Education annual. Charlottesville: Association for the Advancement of Computing Education.
31   Farkas, S. & Johnson, J. (1997). *Teachers talk about Public Education today.* New York: Public Agenda.

32   Mason, A. (2010). Integrating calculators in the secondary Mathematics Classroom: Teachers' attitudes and Perspectives. Retrieved January 01, 2013 from: http://www.eric.ed.gov/.

33   Borris, H. (2004). *Teachers' Instructional Beliefs about integrating Educational Technology.* Retrieved 09 March, 2013 from: http://www. calculators research\teachers belief calculators.htm.

34   Ellington, A. (2003). A meta-analysis of the effects of calculators on students' achievements and attitude levels in precollege mathematics classes. *Journal for Research in Mathematics Education, 34,* 433-463.

35   National Council of Teachers of Mathematics. (2000). *Principles and standards for School Mathematics.* Reston, VA: NCTM, from http:// standards.nctm.org/.
      National Council of Teachers of Mathematics. (2005). *Computation, calculators, and common sense: A position of the National Council of Teachers of Mathematics.* Retrieved September 22, 2010, from http:// www.nctm.org/about/content.aspx?id=6358.

36   Edyburn, D. L. (2006). Cognitive prostheses for students with mild disabilities: Is this what assistive technology looks like? *Journal of Special Education Technology, 21*(4), 62-65.

37   Shuard, H., Walsh, A., Goodwin, J., & Worcester, V. (1991). *Calculators, children and mathematics.* London: Simon and Schuster.

38   Ibid.

39   Hembree, R., & Dessart, D. (1992). Research on calculators in mathematics education in J. Fey and C. Hirsch (eds), *Calculators in Mathematics Education.* Reston VA: National Council of Teachers of Mathematics, 23-32.

40   Maccini, P., & Gagnon, J. C. (2000). Best practices for teaching mathematics to secondary students with special needs. *Focus on Exceptional Children, 32,* 1–22.

41   Edyburn, Cognitive prostheses for students with mild disabilities, 62-65.

42   Horton, S. V., Lovitt, T. C, & White, O. R. (1992). Teaching mathematics to adolescents classified as educable mentally handicapped: Using calculators to remove the computational onus. *Remedial and Special Education, 13,* 36-60.

43   Ibid.

44   Centers for Disease Control. (February 2011). Cognitive impairment: A call for action, now!   https://www.cdc.gov/aging/pdf/ cognitive_impairment/cogimp_poilicy_final.pdf

45   Harvard Extension School Professional Development (HESPD). (2019). Business applications for artificial intelligence: What to know in 2019. https://www. extension.harvard.edu/professional-development/blog/ business-applications-artificial-intelligence-what-know-2019

46   IBM. (2020). Artificial intelligence in medicine. https://www.ibm.com/
     watson-health/learn/artificial-intelligence-medicine
47   Wakefield, K. (2020). Artificial intelligence in business. SAS. https://
     www.sas.com/en_gb/insights/articles/analytics/applications-of-
     artificial-intelligence.html
48   Ibid.
49   Ibid.
50   Ibid.
51   Starr, M. (2018). MIT researchers have created a bizarre
     headset that lets you communicate without speaking.
     Science Alert. (5 April 2018). https://www.sciencealert.com/
     silent-voice-headset-subvocalisation-computer-interface-mit
52   Ibid.
53   IBM. (2020). Artificial intelligence in medicine. https://www.ibm.com/
     watson-health/learn/artificial-intelligence-medicine
54   Ibid.
55   Ibid.
56   Ibid.
57   HESPD, Business applications for artificial intelligence.
58   Ibid.
59   Chiu, M., Henke, N., & Miremade, M. (2018). Most of AI's business
     uses will be in two areas. *Harvard Business Review.* https://hbr.
     org/2018/07/most-of-ais-business-uses-will-be-in-two-areas
60   Wakefield, Artificial Intelligence in Business.
61   Ibid.
62   Ibid.
63   Daugherty, P., & Wilson, J. (2018). *Human + machine: Reimagining
     work in the age of AI.* Boston: Harvard Business Review Press.
64   Equality. (n.d.). Merriam-Webster Online. In Merriam-Webster.
     Retrieved May 1, 2020, from http://www.merriam-webster.com/
     dictionary/equality
65   Equity. (n.d.). Merriam-Webster Online. In Merriam-Webster.
     Retrieved May 1, 2020, from http://www.merriam-webster.com/
     dictionary/equity
66   Fairness. (n.d.). Merriam-Webster Online. In Merriam-Webster.
     Retrieved May 1, 2020, from http://www.merriam-webster.com/
     dictionary/fairness
67   Killen, M. (2018). The origins of morality: Social equality,
     fairness, and justice. *Philosophical Psychology*, 31:5, p. 781. doi:
     10.1080/09515089.2018.1486612
68   Ibid.
69   Masters, G. & R. Adams (2018). What is 'equity' in education?
     Teacher, 30 April 2018. Retrieved from https://www.teachermagazine.
     com.au/columnists/geoff-masters/what-is-equity-in-education
70   Ibid.

71   Ibid.

72   Ibid.

73   Ibid.

74   Kittay, E.F. (2005). At the margins of moral personhood. *Ethics,* 116(1), 100-131. Retrieved from http://www.jstor.org/stable/10.1086/454366

75   Ibid.

76   HESPD, Business applications for artificial intelligence.

77   Ibid.

78   Mayo Clinic Health System. Opthamology Myths & Facts. Retrieved from https://www.mayoclinichealthsystem.org/locations/la-crosse/ services-and-treatments/ophthalmology/myths-and-facts

79   https://futureoflife.org/ai-open-letter/?cn-reloaded=1

80   Tomasello, J., & Brand, B. (2018). *How ESSA and IDEA can support college and career readiness for students with disabilities: Considerations for states.* Washington, DC: American Institutes for Research Youth Policy Forum. Retrieved from https://files.eric.ed.gov/ fulltext/ED586419.pdf

81   The Condition of Education - Preprimary, Elementary, and Secondary Education - Finances - Public School Revenue Sources. *Indicator,* April (2020). (n.d.). Retrieved May 18, 2020, from https://nces.ed.gov/ programs/coe/indicator_cma.asp

82   McWilliams A., Siegel D. (2001). Corporate social responsibility: a theory of the firm perspective. *Academy of Management Review,* 26, 117–127.

83   Bekhouche, I. (2018). Corporate social responsibility in Algeria, the society awareness. *International Affairs and Global Strategy,* 60, 11-21.

84   Ghosh, S., & Shankar, K. (2013). Red, white and pink: Linking public good contributions to private good sales. *Journal of Economic Behavior and Organization,* 88, 96–108.

85   Berens, G., Riel, C., & Bruggen, G. (2005). Corporate associations and consumer product responses: The moderating role of corporate brand dominance. *Journal of Marketing,* 69(3), 35–48.

86   Ghosh, S., & Shankar, K. (2013). *Journal of Economic Behavior & Organization,* 88, 96-108.

87   Klein, P. (2011). The five elements of the best CSR programs. Retrieved May 19, 2020 from https://www.forbes.com/sites/csr/2011/04/26/ the-five-elements-of-the-best-csr-programs/#217e639f4bd5

88   Bright, B. (2008). How more companies are embracing social responsibility as good business. Retrieved May 19, 2020 from http:// www.wsj.com/articles/SB120491426245620011.

89   Unruh, G. (2011). Why CSR is countercyclical. Retrieved May 19, 2020 from https://www.forbes.com/sites/csr/2011/05/16/ why-csr-is-countercyclical/#52c6eba1697f

90   Fleming, L., & Sorenson, O. (2016). Financing by and for the masses. *California Management Review*, 58(2), 5–19.
      Mollick, E. (2014). The dynamics of crowdfunding: An exploratory study. *Journal of Business Venturing*, 29(1), 1–16.

91   Pitschner, S., & Pitschner-Finn, S. (2014). Non-profit differentials in crowd-based financing: Evidence from 50,000 campaigns. *Economics Letters*, 123(3), 391–4.
      Skirnevskiy, V., Bendig, D., & Brettel, M. (2017). The influence of internal social capital on serial creators' success in crowdfunding. *Entrepreneurship Theory and Practice*, 41(2), 209–36.

92   Colombo, M., Franzoni, C., & Rossi-Lamastra, C. (2015). Internal social capital and the attraction of early contributions in crowdfunding. *Entrepreneurship Theory and Practice*, 39(1), 75–100.

93   Ibid.

94   Moore's law: Or how overall processing power for computers will double every two years. Retrieved May 1, 2020 from mooreslaw.org

95   Over 50 Years of Moore's Law. Intel Corporation. Retrieved May 1, 2020 from https://www.intel.com/content/www/us/en/silicon-innovations/moores-law-technology.html

96   Ibid.

97   HESPD, Business applications for artificial intelligence.

98   Ibid.

99   Adaptations. (n.d.) *Special Education Dictionary*. In Special Education Guide. Retrieved May 1, 2020 from https://www.specialeducationguide.com/special-education-dictionary/

100   Ravitch, D. (2007). *Ed speak: A glossary of education terms, phrases, buzzwords and jargon*. Alexandria, VA: Association for Supervision and Curriculum Development, 21.

101   Attention deficit disorder, *Special Education Dictionary*.

102   Attention Deficit/Hyperactivity Disorder, *Special Education Dictionary*.

103   Ravitch, *Ed speak*, 24.

104   Ravitch, *Ed speak*, 48.

105   Cognitive Disability vs. Intellectual Disability. (2018, August 21). Retrieved from https://study.com/academy/lesson/cognitive-disability-vs-intellectual-disability.html.

106   Youman, M., & Mather, N. (2013). Dyslexia laws in the USA. *Annals of Dyslexia*, 63, 133-153.

107   What is dementia? https://www.alz.org/alzheimers-dementia/what-is-dementia

108   What is down syndrome? https://www.cdc.gov/ncbddd/birthdefects/downsyndrome.html

109   Definitions. https://www.dyscalculia.org/

110 Equality. (n.d.). Merriam-Webster Online. In Merriam-Webster. Retrieved May 1, 2020, from http://www.merriam-webster.com/dictionary/equality

111 Equity. (n.d.). Merriam-Webster Online. In Merriam-Webster. Retrieved May 1, 2020, from http://www.merriam-webster.com/dictionary/equity

112 Fairness. (n.d.). Merriam-Webster Online. In Merriam-Webster. Retrieved May 1, 2020, from http://www.merriam-webster.com/dictionary/fairness

113 Cognitive disability vs. intellectual disability. (2018, August 21). Retrieved May 1, 2020 from https://study.com/academy/lesson/cognitive-disability-vs-intellectual-disability.html

114 Special Education Dictionary. Retrieved May 1, 2020 from https://www.specialeducationguide.com/special-education-dictionary/

Made in the USA
Middletown, DE
25 February 2022